SNOW-BOUND

The moon above the eastern wood shone at its full

Snow-Bound

AND OTHER AUTOBIOGRAPHIC POEMS

BY

JOHN GREENLEAF WHITTIER

**Fredonia Books
Amsterdam, The Netherlands**

Snow-Bound and Other Autobiographic Poems

by
John Greenleaf Whittier

ISBN: 1-4101-0232-7

Copyright © 2003 by Fredonia Books

Reprinted from the 1900 edition

Fredonia Books
Amsterdam, The Netherlands
http://www.fredoniabooks.com

All rights reserved, including the right to reproduce this book, or portions thereof, in any form.

In order to make original editions of historical works available to scholars at an economical price, this facsimile of the original edition of 1900 is reproduced from the best available copy and has been digitally enhanced to improve legibility, but the text remains unaltered to retain historical authenticity.

CONTENTS

	PAGE
EDITOR'S NOTE	vii
SNOW-BOUND: A WINTER IDYL	1
THE BAREFOOT BOY	30
TO MY OLD SCHOOLMASTER	34
IN SCHOOL-DAYS	40
MY PLAYMATE	42
MEMORIES	44
TELLING THE BEES	48
BURNS	50
TO MY SISTER	55
ICHABOD	56
THE LOST OCCASION	59
THE QUAKER OF THE OLDEN TIME	62
THE MEETING	63
HAMPTON BEACH	71
A SEA DREAM	74
SUMMER BY THE LAKESIDE	79
SUNSET ON THE BEARCAMP	83
THE LAST WALK IN AUTUMN	86
AN OUT-DOOR RECEPTION	95
THE TENT ON THE BEACH	99
The Wreck of Rivermouth	108
The Grave by the Lake	114
The Brother of Mercy	126
The Changeling	129
The Maids of Attitash	134
Kallundborg Church	140
The Cable Hymn	144
The Dead Ship of Harpswell	146
The Palatine	149
Abraham Davenport	154
The Worship of Nature	158

CONTENTS

Ego	160
My Psalm	166
Response	169
At Last	170
Notes	173

EDITOR'S NOTE

WHEN Mr. Whittier, a few years before his death, supervised the definitive Riverside edition of his Poems, he classified them under several heads, among them being "Poems Subjective and Reminiscent." In this group he placed "Snow-Bound," "Memories," "Ego," "The Barefoot Boy," "My Psalm," "In School-Days," "Response," "To my Sister," and others which were now disclosures of himself with the frankness of a Friend bearing testimony, now vivid recollections of the early years of his life; for as with poets in general, Memory often beckoned Imagination to come and sit in the cool shade of youth.

Though this section of his Poems is thus purposely autobiographic in character, all of the divisions, "Personal," "Anti-Slavery," "Poems of Nature," "Songs of Labor and Reform," "Religious Poems," "Narrative and Legendary Poems," "Occasional Poems," "At Sundown," are characterized by that strong personal element which has endeared Whittier to readers because the man, genuinely humble in spirit, was yet so at one with God, nature, and humanity that he spoke and sang clearly in his own voice, never in falsetto, always as one upon whom as on an instrument the spirit of truth played from the lowest note to the top of his compass.

Never was a poet so frank and so entirely void of self-conceit. If sometimes he rambled on in verse about the thoughts and feelings over which he brooded till one wondered that he should find himself so interesting, there never was a note of vanity or even of the pride of humility. The forthrightness of his song might sometimes be careless, perhaps garrulous in form, but it was always genuine and not assumed; certainly it was the farthest removed from dramatic concealment. These qualities make the man himself so evident in his verse that it is doubtful if his biography will ever be much read; his life is so much more vividly told in his own poems than it ever could be by any other narrator, even than it could have been by himself in prose. Indeed, there is a curious corroboration of this in Mr. Pickard's *Life*. There the biographer has collected some of Mr. Whittier's letters, and how bald, how dry are these expressions of himself beside the animated clear-voiced and liquid notes of his song!

The mere incidents of the poet's life, though he lived in stirring times and was a most active instrument in creating the stir, are devoid of dramatic character. No wood-thrush could seem so concealed from observation as this "wood-thrush of Essex." The simple household life he led, under conditions often of physical weakness, was in strange contrast to the clarion bursts with which in a spiritual sense he led forth the hosts to war. No, one must look for the real Whittier not in the annals of Amesbury, but in the poems which re-

EDITOR'S NOTE

corded the life of a great spirit at once homely and universal, sensitive to the lightest breath yet animated by heroic virtues, now domiciled by a country hearth, now at large by ocean and mountain or fighting on foot in the ranks of the great army engaged in the Holy War.

This volume is planned with the purpose of giving an outline, in Whittier's own most characteristic verse, of the life of this truthful poet. An outline only it can be, yet by means of it one may trace in no uncertain phrase the New England boy baptized by the spirit of the Society of Friends, yet dominated by an imagination which made the world glow for him in color and sing with a melody not to be drowned by the voices of wrath which were rising all about him. In "Snow-Bound" and in "The Barefoot Boy" the very details of his homely life are drawn with an accuracy rightly called Flemish rather than pre-Raphaelite, because of the rich human flavor attached to it. The poems which follow touch upon deeper experiences, scarcely uncovered except in verse, yet there almost intimately revealed. In "Burns" one may read the poet's own confession of how the Scotch singer, so akin to him in many ways, was the touchstone by which he discovered the purity of the vein which ran through his own formation. The two poems on Webster are chosen out of all the number properly relating to the anti-slavery crusade, because they combine in so emphatic a manner that stern temper as of a Hebrew prophet with which Whittier spoke his "Thus saith the Lord," and that utter absence of vindictiveness which made him walk unscathed in the midst of his own words of fire; because also they hint at that strong political temper which gave the poet a singularly practical hold upon the movements of his day.

It is not an abrupt passage from Whittier the anti-slavery prophet to Whittier the Friend and seer, and then in a group of half a dozen poems one may catch some glimpse of that affectionate knowledge of nature, bounded by the ocean on one side and the mountains on the other, which shows, almost more surely than any other phase of his poetical spirit, the large, universal temper of a man walking with the Lord God in the garden in the cool of the day. But by a natural transition the reader comes at once on this genuinely companionable being in happy converse with friends. In actual life Whittier, shy and reserved, seemed to meet others most frankly out of doors. "An Outdoor Reception" is almost a chronicle of the many picnics in which he engaged, but the mosaic "The Tent on the Beach" is as characteristic a picture of the man Whittier in the midst of his congenial companions, as "Snow-Bound" is of the boy in the seclusion of home. "The Tent on the Beach," moreover, offers a happy illustration of the storytelling faculty which was native to the poet, and has made him on the whole the nearest to the primitive ballad singer of any of our poets.

And so finally we may listen to the poet by himself in those reflective verses, mellow with an age calm and cheerful, that sing his serene creed and

EDITOR'S NOTE

show most directly and simply his place in the choir invisible. It would be easy to fill out this outline at almost every point, but outline though it is, here is a picture drawn by himself of the most human and artless and yet self-informed of our poets.

The head-notes to the poems are those prefixed by the poet himself when collecting the Riverside edition, and transferred by the editor, with occasional slight enlargement or modification, when preparing the Cambridge edition.

H. E. S.

SNOW-BOUND

INTRODUCTORY NOTE

THE inmates of the family at the Whittier homestead who are referred to in the poem were my father, mother, my brother and two sisters, and my uncle and aunt, both unmarried. In addition, there was the district school master, who boarded with us. The "not unfeared, half-welcome guest" was Harriet Livermore, daughter of Judge Livermore, of New Hampshire, a young woman of fine natural ability, enthusiastic, eccentric, with slight control over her violent temper, which sometimes made her religious profession doubtful. She was equally ready to exhort in school-house prayer-meetings and dance in a Washington ball-room, while her father was a member of Congress. She early embraced the doctrine of the Second Advent, and felt it her duty to proclaim the Lord's speedy coming. With this message she crossed the Atlantic and spent the greater part of a long life in travelling over Europe and Asia. She lived some time with Lady Hester Stanhope, a woman as fantastic and mentally strained as herself, on the slope of Mt. Lebanon, but finally quarrelled with her in regard to two white horses with red marks on their backs which suggested the idea of saddles, on which her titled hostess expected to ride into Jerusalem with the Lord. A friend of mine found her, when quite an old woman, wandering in Syria with a tribe of Arabs, who with the Oriental notion that madness is inspiration, accepted her as their prophetess and leader. At the time referred to in *Snow-Bound* she was boarding at the Rocks Village, about two miles from us.

In my boyhood, in our lonely farm-house, we had scanty sources of information; few books and only a small weekly newspaper. Our only annual was the Almanac. Under such circumstances story-telling was a necessary resource in the long winter evenings. My father when a young man had traversed the wilderness to Canada, and could tell us of his adventures with Indians and wild beasts, and of his sojourn in the French villages. My uncle was ready with his record of hunting and fishing and, it must be confessed, with stories which he at least half believed, of witchcraft and apparitions. My mother, who was born in the Indian-haunted region of Somersworth, New Hampshire, between Dover and Portsmouth, told us of the inroads of the savages, and the narrow escape of her ancestors. She described strange people who lived on the Piscataqua and Cocheco, among whom was Bantam, the sorcerer. I have in my possession the wizard's "conjuring book," which he solemnly opened when consulted. It is a copy of Cornelius Agrippa's *Magic*, printed in 1651, dedicated to Dr. Robert Child, who, like Michael Scott, had learned

> "the art of glammorie
> In Padua beyond the sea,"

and who is famous in the annals of Massachusetts, where he was at one time a resident, as the first man who dared petition the General Court for liberty of conscience. The full title of the book is *Three Books of Occult Philosophy, by Henry Cornelius Agrippa, Knight, Doctor of both Laws, Counsellor to Cæsar's Sacred Majesty and Judge of the Prerogative Court.*

SNOW-BOUND

A WINTER IDYL

TO THE MEMORY OF THE HOUSEHOLD IT DE-
SCRIBES

THIS POEM IS DEDICATED BY THE AUTHOR.

"As the Spirits of Darkness be stronger in the dark, so Good Spirits, which be Angels of Light, are augmented not only by the Divine light of the Sun, but also by our common VVood Fire: and as the Celestial Fire drives away dark spirits, so also this our Fire of VVood doth the same." — COR. AGRIPPA, *Occult Philosophy*, Book I. ch. v.

"Announced by all the trumpets of the sky,
Arrives the snow, and, driving o'er the fields,
Seems nowhere to alight: the whited air
Hides hills and woods, the river and the heaven,
And veils the farm-house at the garden's end.
The sled and traveller stopped, the courier's feet
Delayed, all friends shut out, the housemates sit
Around the radiant fireplace, enclosed
In a tumultuous privacy of storm."
                    EMERSON, *The Snow Storm.*

THE sun that brief December day
  Rose cheerless over hills of gray,
And, darkly circled, gave at noon
A sadder light than waning moon.

Slow tracing down the thickening sky
Its mute and ominous prophecy,
A portent seeming less than threat,
It sank from sight before it set.
A chill no coat, however stout,
Of homespun stuff could quite shut out,
A hard, dull bitterness of cold,
That checked, mid-vein, the circling race
Of life-blood in the sharpened face,
The coming of the snow-storm told.
The wind blew east; we heard the roar
Of Ocean on his wintry shore,
And felt the strong pulse throbbing there
Beat with low rhythm our inland air.

Meanwhile we did our nightly chores, —
Brought in the wood from out of doors,
Littered the stalls, and from the mows
Raked down the herd's-grass for the cows
Heard the horse whinnying for his corn;
And, sharply clashing horn on horn,
Impatient down the stanchion rows
The cattle shake their walnut bows;
While, peering from his early perch
Upon the scaffold's pole of birch,
The cock his crested helmet bent
And down his querulous challenge sent.

Unwarmed by any sunset light
The gray day darkened into night,
A night made hoary with the swarm
And whirl-dance of the blinding storm,

As zigzag, wavering to and fro,
Crossed and recrossed the wingèd snow:
And ere the early bedtime came
The white drift piled the window-frame,
And through the glass the clothes-line posts
Looked in like tall and sheeted ghosts.

So all night long the storm roared on:
The morning broke without a sun;
In tiny spherule traced with lines
Of Nature's geometric signs,
In starry flake, and pellicle,
All day the hoary meteor fell;
And, when the second morning shone,
We looked upon a world unknown,
On nothing we could call our own.
Around the glistening wonder bent
The blue walls of the firmament,
No cloud above, no earth below, —
A universe of sky and snow!
The old familiar sights of ours
Took marvellous shapes; strange domes and
    towers
Rose up where sty or corn-crib stood,
Or garden-wall, or belt of wood;
A smooth white mound the brush-pile showed,
A fenceless drift what once was road;
The bridle-post an old man sat
With loose-flung coat and high cocked hat;
The well-curb had a Chinese roof;
And even the long sweep, high aloof,
In its slant splendor, seemed to tell
Of Pisa's leaning miracle.

A prompt, decisive man, no breath
Our father wasted: "Boys, a path!"
Well pleased, (for when did farmer boy
Count such a summons less than joy?)
Our buskins on our feet we drew;
With mittened hands, and caps drawn low
To guard our necks and ears from snow,
We cut the solid whiteness through.
And, where the drift was deepest, made
A tunnel walled and overlaid
With dazzling crystal: we had read
Of rare Aladdin's wondrous cave,
And to our own his name we gave,
With many a wish the luck were ours
To test his lamp's supernal powers.
We reached the barn with merry din,
And roused the prisoned brutes within.
The old horse thrust his long head out,
And grave with wonder gazed about;
The cock his lusty greeting said,
And forth his speckled harem led;
The oxen lashed their tails, and hooked,
And mild reproach of hunger looked;
The hornèd patriarch of the sheep,
Like Egypt's Amun roused from sleep,
Shook his sage head with gesture mute,
And emphasized with stamp of foot.

All day the gusty north-wind bore
The loosening drift its breath before;
Low circling round its southern zone,
The sun through dazzling snow-mist shone

No church-bell lent its Christian tone
To the savage air, no social smoke
Curled over woods of snow-hung oak.
A solitude made more intense
By dreary-voicèd elements,
The shrieking of the mindless wind,
The moaning tree-boughs swaying blind,
And on the glass the unmeaning beat
Of ghostly finger-tips of sleet.
Beyond the circle of our hearth
No welcome sound of toil or mirth
Unbound the spell, and testified
Of human life and thought outside.
We minded that the sharpest ear
The buried brooklet could not hear,
The music of whose liquid lip
Had been to us companionship,
And, in our lonely life, had grown
To have an almost human tone.

As night drew on, and, from the crest
Of wooded knolls that ridged the west,
The sun, a snow-blown traveller, sank
From sight beneath the smothering bank,
We piled, with care, our nightly stack
Of wood against the chimney-back, —
The oaken log, green, huge, and thick,
And on its top the stout back-stick;
The knotty forestick laid apart,
And filled between with curious art
The ragged brush; then, hovering near,
We watched the first red blaze appear,

Heard the sharp crackle, caught the gleam
On whitewashed wall and sagging beam,
Until the old, rude-furnished room
Burst, flower-like, into rosy bloom;
While radiant with a mimic flame
Outside the sparkling drift became,
And through the bare-boughed lilac-tree
Our own warm hearth seemed blazing free.
The crane and pendent trammels showed,
The Turks' heads on the andirons glowed;
While childish fancy, prompt to tell
The meaning of the miracle,
Whispered the old rhyme: "*Under the tree
When fire outdoor burns merrily,
There the witches are making tea.*"

The moon above the eastern wood
Shone at its full; the hill-range stood
Transfigured in the silver flood,
Its blown snows flashing cold and keen,
Dead white, save where some sharp ravine
Took shadow, or the sombre green
Of hemlocks turned to pitchy black
Against the whiteness at their back.
For such a world and such a night
Most fitting that unwarming light,
Which only seemed where'er it fell
To make the coldness visible.

Shut in from all the world without,
We sat the clean-winged hearth about,
Content to let the north-wind roar
In baffled rage at pane and door,

While the red logs before us beat
The frost-line back with tropic heat;
And ever, when a louder blast
Shook beam and rafter as it passed,
The merrier up its roaring draught
The great throat of the chimney laughed;
The house-dog on his paws outspread
Laid to the fire his drowsy head,
The cat's dark silhouette on the wall
A couchant tiger's seemed to fall;
And, for the winter fireside meet,
Between the andirons' straddling feet,
The mug of cider simmered slow,
The apples sputtered in a row,
And, close at hand, the basket stood
With nuts from brown October's wood.

What matter how the night behaved?
What matter how the north-wind raved?
Blow high, blow low, not all its snow
Could quench our hearth-fire's ruddy glow.
O Time and Change! — with hair as gray
As was my sire's that winter day,
How strange it seems, with so much gone
Of life and love, to still live on!
Ah, brother! only I and thou
Are left of all that circle now, —
The dear home faces whereupon
That fitful firelight paled and shone.
Henceforward, listen as we will,
The voices of that hearth are still;
Look where we may, the wide earth o'er,
Those lighted faces smile no more.

We tread the paths their feet have worn,
　　We sit beneath their orchard trees,
　　We hear, like them, the hum of bees
And rustle of the bladed corn;
We turn the pages that they read,
　　Their written words we linger o'er,
But in the sun they cast no shade,
No voice is heard, no sign is made,
　　No step is on the conscious floor!
Yet Love will dream, and Faith will trust
(Since He who knows our need is just,)
That somehow, somewhere, meet we must.
Alas for him who never sees
The stars shine through his cypress-trees!
Who, hopeless, lays his dead away,
Nor looks to see the breaking day
Across the mournful marbles play!
Who hath not learned, in hours of faith,
　　The truth to flesh and sense unknown,
That Life is ever lord of Death,
　　And Love can never lose its own!

We sped the time with stories old,
Wrought puzzles out, and riddles told,
Or stammered from our school-book lore
"The Chief of Gambia's golden shore."
How often since, when all the land
Was clay in Slavery's shaping hand,
As if a far-blown trumpet stirred
The languorous sin-sick air, I heard:
"*Does not the voice of reason cry,*
　　Claim the first right which Nature gave,

From the red scourge of bondage fly,
  Nor deign to live a burdened slave!"
Our father rode again his ride
On Memphremagog's wooded side;
Sat down again to moose and samp
In trapper's hut and Indian camp;
Lived o'er the old idyllic ease
Beneath St. François' hemlock-trees;
Again for him the moonlight shone
On Norman cap and bodiced zone;
Again he heard the violin play
Which led the village dance away.
And mingled in its merry whirl
The grandam and the laughing girl.
Or, nearer home, our steps he led
Where Salisbury's level marshes spread
  Mile-wide as flies the laden bee;
Where merry mowers, hale and strong,
Swept, scythe on scythe, their swaths along
  The low green prairies of the sea.
We shared the fishing off Boar's Head,
  And round the rocky Isles of Shoals
  The hake-broil on the drift-wood coals;
The chowder on the sand-beach made,
Dipped by the hungry, steaming hot,
With spoons of clam-shell from the pot.
We heard the tales of witchcraft old,
And dream and sign and marvel told
To sleepy listeners as they lay
Stretched idly on the salted hay,
Adrift along the winding shores,
When favoring breezes deigned to blow

The square sail of the gundelow
And idle lay the useless oars.

Our mother, while she turned her wheel
Or run the new-knit stocking-heel,
Told how the Indian hordes came down
At midnight on Cocheco town,
And how her own great-uncle bore
His cruel scalp-mark to fourscore.
Recalling, in her fitting phrase,
 So rich and picturesque and free,
 (The common unrhymed poetry
Of simple life and country ways,)
The story of her early days, —
She made us welcome to her home;
Old hearths grew wide to give us room;
We stole with her a frightened look
At the gray wizard's conjuring-book,
The fame whereof went far and wide
Through all the simple country side;
We heard the hawks at twilight play,
The boat-horn on Piscataqua,
The loon's weird laughter far away;
We fished her little trout-brook, knew
What flowers in wood and meadow grew,
What sunny hillsides autumn-brown
She climbed to shake the ripe nuts down,
Saw where in sheltered cove and bay
The ducks' black squadron anchored lay,
And heard the wild-geese calling loud
Beneath the gray November cloud.

Then, haply, with a look more grave,
And soberer tone, some tale she gave
From painful Sewel's ancient tome,
Beloved in every Quaker home,
Of faith fire-winged by martyrdom,
Or Chalkley's Journal, old and quaint, —
Gentlest of skippers, rare sea-saint! —
Who, when the dreary calms prevailed,
And water-butt and bread-cask failed,
And cruel, hungry eyes pursued
His portly presence mad for food,
With dark hints muttered under breath
Of casting lots for life or death,
Offered, if Heaven withheld supplies,
To be himself the sacrifice.
Then, suddenly, as if to save
The good man from his living grave,
A ripple on the water grew,
A school of porpoise flashed in view.
Take, eat," he said, " and be content;
These fishes in my stead are sent
By Him who gave the tangled ram
To spare the child of Abraham."

Our uncle, innocent of books,
Was rich in lore of fields and brooks,
The ancient teachers never dumb
Of nature's unhoused lyceum.
In moons and tides and weather wise,
He read the clouds as prophecies,
And foul or fair could well divine,
By many an occult hint and sign,

Holding the cunning-warded keys
To all the woodcraft mysteries;
Himself to Nature's heart so near
That all her voices in his ear
Of beast or bird had meanings clear,
Like Apollonius of old,
Who knew the tales the sparrows told,
Or Hermes who interpreted
What the sage cranes of Nilus said;
A simple, guileless, childlike man,
Content to live where life began;
Strong only on his native grounds,
The little world of sights and sounds
Whose girdle was the parish bounds,
Whereof his fondly partial pride
The common features magnified,
As Surrey hills to mountains grew
In White of Selborne's loving view, —
He told how teal and loon he shot,
And how the eagle's eggs he got,
The feats on pond and river done,
The prodigies of rod and gun;
Till, warming with the tales he told,
Forgotten was the outside cold,
The bitter wind unheeded blew,
From ripening corn the pigeons flew,
The partridge drummed i' the wood, the mink
Went fishing down the river-brink.
In fields with bean or clover gay,
The woodchuck, like a hermit gray,

  Peered from the doorway of his cell;
The muskrat plied the mason's trade,

And tier by tier his mud-walls laid;
And from the shagbark overhead
  The grizzled squirrel dropped his shell.

Next, the dear aunt, whose smile of cheer
And voice in dreams I see and hear, —
The sweetest woman ever Fate
Perverse denied a household mate,
Who, lonely, homeless, not the less
Found peace in love's unselfishness,
And welcome wheresoe'er she went,
A calm and gracious element,
Whose presence seemed the sweet income
And womanly atmosphere of home, —
Called up her girlhood memories,
The huskings and the apple-bees,
The sleigh-rides and the summer sails,
Weaving through all the poor details
And homespun warp of circumstance
A golden woof-thread of romance.
For well she kept her genial mood
And simple faith of maidenhood;
Before her still a cloud-land lay,
The mirage loomed across her way;
The morning dew, that dries so soon
With others, glistened at her noon;
Through years of toil and soil and care,
From glossy tress to thin gray hair,
All unprofaned she held apart
The virgin fancies of the heart.
Be shame to him of woman born
Who hath for such but thought of scorn.

There, too, our elder sister plied
Her evening task the stand beside;
A full, rich nature, free to trust,
Truthful and almost sternly just,
Impulsive, earnest, prompt to act,
And make her generous thought a fact,
Keeping with many a light disguise
The secret of self-sacrifice.
O heart sore-tried! thou hast the best
That Heaven itself could give thee, — rest,
Rest from all bitter thoughts and things!
　How many a poor one's blessing went
　With thee beneath the low green tent
Whose curtain never outward swings!

As one who held herself a part
Of all she saw, and let her heart
　Against the household bosom lean,
Upon the motley-braided mat
Our youngest and our dearest sat,
Lifting her large, sweet, asking eyes,
　Now bathed in the unfading green
And holy peace of Paradise.
Oh, looking from some heavenly hill,
　Or from the shade of saintly palms,
　Or silver reach of river calms,
Do those large eyes behold me still?
With me one little year ago: —
The chill weight of the winter snow
　For months upon her grave has lain;
And now, when summer south-winds blow
　And brier and harebell bloom again,

I tread the pleasant paths we trod,
I see the violet-sprinkled sod
Whereon she leaned, too frail and weak
The hillside flowers she loved to seek,
Yet following me where'er I went
With dark eyes full of love's content.
The birds are glad; the brier-rose fills
The air with sweetness; all the hills
Stretch green to June's unclouded sky;
But still I wait with ear and eye
For something gone which should be nigh,
A loss in all familiar things,
In flower that blooms, and bird that sings.
And yet, dear heart! remembering thee,
    Am I not richer than of old?
Safe in thy immortality,
    What change can reach the wealth I hold?
    What chance can mar the pearl and gold
Thy love hath left in trust with me?
And while in life's late afternoon,
    Where cool and long the shadows grow,
I walk to meet the night that soon
    Shall shape and shadow overflow,
I cannot feel that thou art far,
Since near at need the angels are;
And when the sunset gates unbar,
    Shall I not see thee waiting stand,
And, white against the evening star,
The welcome of thy beckoning hand?

Brisk wielder of the birch and rule,
The master of the district school

Held at the fire his favored place;
Its warm glow lit a laughing face
Fresh-hued and fair, where scarce appeared
The uncertain prophecy of beard.
He teased the mitten-blinded cat,
Played cross-pins on my uncle's hat,
Sang songs, and told us what befalls
In classic Dartmouth's college halls.
Born the wild Northern hills among,
From whence his yeoman father wrung
By patient toil subsistence scant,
Not competence and yet not want,
He early gained the power to pay
His cheerful, self-reliant way;
Could doff at ease his scholar's gown
To peddle wares from town to town;
Or through the long vacation's reach
In lonely lowland districts teach,
Where all the droll experience found
At stranger hearths in boarding round,
The moonlit skater's keen delight,
The sleigh-drive through the frosty night,
The rustic-party, with its rough
Accompaniment of blind-man's-buff,
And whirling-plate, and forfeits paid,
His winter task a pastime made.
Happy the snow-locked homes wherein
He tuned his merry violin,
Or played the athlete in the barn,
Or held the good dame's winding-yarn,
Or mirth-provoking versions told
Of classic legends rare and old,

Wherein the scenes of Greece and Rome
Had all the commonplace of home,
And little seemed at best the odds
'Twixt Yankee pedlers and old gods;
Where Pindus-born Arachthus took
The guise of any grist-mill brook,
And dread Olympus at his will
Became a huckleberry hill.

A careless boy that night he seemed;
  But at his desk he had the look
And air of one who wisely schemed,
  And hostage from the future took
  In trainèd thought and lore of book.
Large-brained, clear-eyed, of such as he
Shall Freedom's young apostles be,
Who, following in War's bloody trail,
Shall every lingering wrong assail;
All chains from limb and spirit strike,
Uplift the black and white alike;
Scatter before their swift advance
The darkness and the ignorance,
The pride, the lust, the squalid sloth,
Which nurtured Treason's monstrous growth,
Made murder pastime, and the hell
Of prison-torture possible;
The cruel lie of caste refute,
Old forms remould, and substitute
For Slavery's lash the freeman's will,
For blind routine, wise-handed skill;
A school-house plant on every hill,
Stretching in radiate nerve-lines thence
The quick wires of intelligence;

Till North and South together brought
Shall own the same electric thought,
In peace a common flag salute,
And, side by side in labor's free
And unresentful rivalry,
Harvest the fields wherein they fought.

Another guest that winter night
Flashed back from lustrous eyes the light.
Unmarked by time, and yet not young,
The honeyed music of her tongue
And words of meekness scarcely told
A nature passionate and bold,
Strong, self-concentred, spurning guide,
Its milder features dwarfed beside
Her unbent will's majestic pride.
She sat among us, at the best,
A not unfeared, half-welcome guest,
Rebuking with her cultured phrase
Our homeliness of words and ways.
A certain pard-like, treacherous grace
Swayed the lithe limbs and dropped the lash
Lent the white teeth their dazzling flash;
And under low brows, black with night,
Rayed out at times a dangerous light;
The sharp heat-lightnings of her face
Presaging ill to him whom Fate
Condemned to share her love or hate.
A woman tropical, intense
In thought and act, in soul and sense,
She blended in a like degree
The vixen and the devotee.

Revealing with each freak or feint
  The temper of Petruchio's Kate,
The raptures of Siena's saint.
Her tapering hand and rounded wrist
Had facile power to form a fist;
The warm, dark languish of her eyes
Was never safe from wrath's surprise.
Brows saintly calm and lips devout
Knew every change of scowl and pout;
And the sweet voice had notes more high
And shrill for social battle-cry.

Since then what old cathedral town
Has missed her pilgrim staff and gown,
What convent-gate has held its lock
Against the challenge of her knock!
Through Smyrna's plague-hushed thoroughfares,
Up sea-set Malta's rocky stairs,
Gray olive slopes of hills that hem
Thy tombs and shrines, Jerusalem,
Or startling on her desert throne
The crazy Queen of Lebanon
With claims fantastic as her own,
Her tireless feet have held their way;
And still, unrestful, bowed, and gray,
She watches under Eastern skies,
  With hope each day renewed and fresh,
  The Lord's quick coming in the flesh,
Whereof she dreams and prophesies!

Where'er her troubled path may be,
  The Lord's sweet pity with her go!

The outward wayward life we see,
  The hidden springs we may not know.
Nor is it given us to discern
  What threads the fatal sisters spun,
  Through what ancestral years has run
The sorrow with the woman born,
What forged her cruel chain of moods,
What set her feet in solitudes
  And held the love within her mute,
What mingled madness in the blood,
  A life-long discord and annoy,
  Water of tears with oil of joy,
And hid within the folded bud
  Perversities of flower and fruit.
It is not ours to separate
  The tangled skein of will and fate,
To show what metes and bounds should stand
Upon the soul's debatable land,
And between choice and Providence
Divide the circle of events;
But He who knows our frame is just,
Merciful and compassionate,
And full of sweet assurances
And hope for all the language is,
That He remembereth we are dust!

At last the great logs, crumbling low,
Sent out a dull and duller glow,
The bull's-eye watch that hung in view,
Ticking its weary circuit through,
Pointed with mutely warning sign
Its black hand to the hour of nine.

That sign the pleasant circle broke :
My uncle ceased his pipe to smoke,
Knocked from its bowl the refuse gray,
And laid it tenderly away;
Then roused himself to safely cover
The dull red brands with ashes over.
And while, with care, our mother laid
The work aside, her steps she stayed
One moment, seeking to express
Her grateful sense of happiness
For food and shelter, warmth and health,
And love's contentment more than wealth,
With simple wishes (not the weak,
Vain prayers which no fulfilment seek,
But such as warm the generous heart,
O'er-prompt to do with Heaven its part)
That none might lack, that bitter night,
For bread and clothing, warmth and light.

Within our beds awhile we heard
The wind that round the gables roared,
With now and then a ruder shock,
Which made our very bedsteads rock.
We heard the loosened clapboards tost,
The board-nails snapping in the frost;
And on us, through the unplastered wall,
Felt the light sifted snow-flakes fall.
But sleep stole on, as sleep will do
When hearts are light and life is new;
Faint and more faint the murmurs grew,
Till in the summer-land of dreams
They softened to the sound of streams,

Low stir of leaves, and dip of oars,
And lapsing waves on quiet shores.

Next morn we wakened with the shout
Of merry voices high and clear;
And saw the teamsters drawing near
To break the drifted highways out.
Down the long hillside treading slow
We saw the half-buried oxen go,
Shaking the snow from heads uptost,
Their straining nostrils white with frost.
Before our door the straggling train
Drew up, an added team to gain.
The elders threshed their hands a-cold,
   Passed, with the cider-mug, their jokes
   From lip to lip; the younger folks
Down the loose snow-banks, wrestling, rolled
Then toiled again the cavalcade
   O'er windy hill, through clogged ravine,
   And woodland paths that wound between
Low drooping pine-boughs winter-weighed.
From every barn a team afoot,
At every house a new recruit,
Where, drawn by Nature's subtlest law,
Haply the watchful young men saw
Sweet doorway pictures of the curls
And curious eyes of merry girls,
Lifting their hands in mock defence
Against the snow-ball's compliments,
And reading in each missive tost
The charm with Eden never lost.

We heard once more the sleigh-bells' sound;
   And, following where the teamsters led,
The wise old Doctor went his round,
Just pausing at our door to say,
In the brief autocratic way
Of one who, prompt at Duty's call,
Was free to urge her claim on all,
   That some poor neighbor sick abed
At night our mother's aid would need.
For, one in generous thought and deed,
   What mattered in the sufferer's sight,
   The Quaker matron's inward light,
The Doctor's mail of Calvin's creed?
All hearts confess the saints elect
   Who, twain in faith, in love agree,
And melt not in an acid sect
   The Christian pearl of charity!

So days went on: a week had passed
Since the great world was heard from last.
The Almanac we studied o'er,
Read and reread our little store
Of books and pamphlets, scarce a score;
One harmless novel, mostly hid
From younger eyes, a book forbid,
And poetry, (or good or bad,
A single book was all we had,)
Where Ellwood's meek, drab-skirted Muse,
   A stranger to the heathen Nine,
   Sang, with a somewhat nasal whine,
The wars of David and the Jews.
At last the floundering carrier bore
The village paper to our door.

Lo! broadening outward as we read,
To warmer zones the horizon spread;
In panoramic length unrolled
We saw the marvels that it told.
Before us passed the painted Creeks,
  And daft McGregor on his raids
  In Costa Rica's everglades.
And up Taygetos winding slow
Rode Ypsilanti's Mainote Greeks,
A Turk's head at each saddle-bow!
Welcome to us its week-old news,
Its corner for the rustic Muse,
  Its monthly gauge of snow and rain,
Its record, mingling in a breath
The wedding bell and dirge of death:
Jest, anecdote, and love-lorn tale,
The latest culprit sent to jail;
Its hue and cry of stolen and lost,
Its vendue sales and goods at cost,
  And traffic calling loud for gain.
We felt the stir of hall and street,
The pulse of life that round us beat;
The chill embargo of the snow
Was melted in the genial glow;
Wide swung again our ice-locked door,
And all the world was ours once more!

Clasp, Angel of the backward look
  And folded wings of ashen gray
  And voice of echoes far away,
The brazen covers of thy book;
The weird palimpsest old and vast,

Wherein thou hid'st the spectral past;
Where, closely mingling, pale and glow
The characters of joy and woe;
The monographs of outlived years,
Or smile-illumed or dim with tears,
  Green hills of life that slope to death,
And haunts of home, whose vistaed trees
Shade off to mournful cypresses
  With the white amaranths underneath.
Even while I look, I can but heed
  The restless sands' incessant fall,
Importunate hours that hours succeed,
Each clamorous with its own sharp need,
  And duty keeping pace with all.
Shut down and clasp the heavy lids;
I hear again the voice that bids
The dreamer leave his dream midway
For larger hopes and graver fears:
Life greatens in these later years,
The century's aloe flowers to-day!

Yet, haply, in some lull of life,
Some Truce of God which breaks its strife,
The worldling's eyes shall gather dew,
  Dreaming in throngful city ways
Of winter joys his boyhood knew;
And dear and early friends — the few
Who yet remain — shall pause to view
  These Flemish pictures of old days;
Sit with me by the homestead hearth,
And stretch the hands of memory forth
To warm them at the wood-fire's blaze!

And thanks untraced to lips unknown
Shall greet me like the odors blown
From unseen meadows newly mown,
Or lilies floating in some pond,
Wood-fringed, the wayside gaze beyond
The traveller owns the grateful sense
Of sweetness near, he knows not whence
And, pausing, takes with forehead bare
The benediction of the air.

THE BAREFOOT BOY

BLESSINGS on thee, little man,
  Barefoot boy, with cheek of tan !
With thy turned-up pantaloons,
And thy merry whistled tunes;
With thy red lip, redder still
Kissed by strawberries on the hill;
With the sunshine on thy face,
Through thy torn brim's jaunty grace
From my heart I give thee joy, —
I was once a barefoot boy !
Prince thou art, — the grown-up man
Only is republican.
Let the million-dollared ride !
Barefoot, trudging at his side,
Thou hast more than he can buy
In the reach of ear and eye, —
Outward sunshine, inward joy:
Blessings on thee, barefoot boy !

THE BAREFOOT BOY

Oh for boyhood's painless play,
Sleep that wakes in laughing day,
Health that mocks the doctor's rules,
Knowledge never learned of schools,
Of the wild bee's morning chase,
Of the wild-flower's time and place,
Flight of fowl and habitude
Of the tenants of the wood;
How the tortoise bears his shell,
How the woodchuck digs his cell,
And the ground-mole sinks his well;
How the robin feeds her young,
How the oriole's nest is hung;
Where the whitest lilies blow,
Where the freshest berries grow,
Where the ground-nut trails its vine,
Where the wood-grape's clusters shine;
Of the black wasp's cunning way,
Mason of his walls of clay,
And the architectural plans
Of gray hornet artisans!
For, eschewing books and tasks,
Nature answers all he asks;
Hand in hand with her he walks,
Face to face with her he talks,
Part and parcel of her joy, —
Blessings on the barefoot boy!

Oh for boyhood's time of June,
Crowding years in one brief moon,
When all things I heard or saw,
Me, their master, waited for.

THE BAREFOOT BOY

I was rich in flowers and trees,
Humming-birds and honey-bees;
For my sport the squirrel played,
Plied the snouted mole his spade;
For my taste the blackberry cone
Purpled over hedge and stone;
Laughed the brook for my delight
Through the day and through the night
Whispering at the garden wall,
Talked with me from fall to fall;
Mine the sand-rimmed pickerel pond,
Mine the walnut slopes beyond,
Mine, on bending orchard trees,
Apples of Hesperides!
Still as my horizon grew,
Larger grew my riches too;
All the world I saw or knew
Seemed a complex Chinese toy,
Fashioned for a barefoot boy!

Oh for festal dainties spread,
Like my bowl of milk and bread;
Pewter spoon and bowl of wood,
On the door-stone, gray and rude!
O'er me, like a regal tent,
Cloudy-ribbed, the sunset bent,
Purple-curtained, fringed with gold,
Looped in many a wind-swung fold;
While for music came the play
Of the pied frogs' orchestra;
And, to light the noisy choir,
Lit the fly his lamp of fire.

THE BAREFOOT BOY

I was monarch: pomp and joy
Waited on the barefoot boy!

Cheerily, then, my little man,
Live and laugh, as boyhood can!
Though the flinty slopes be hard,
Stubble-speared the new-mown sward,
Every morn shall lead thee through
Fresh baptisms of the dew;
Every evening from thy feet
Shall the cool wind kiss the heat:
All too soon these feet must hide
In the prison cells of pride,
Lose the freedom of the sod,
Like a colt's for work be shod,
Made to tread the mills of toil,
Up and down in ceaseless moil:
Happy if their track be found
Never on forbidden ground;
Happy if they sink not in
Quick and treacherous sands of sin.
Ah! that thou couldst know thy joy,
Ere it passes, barefoot boy!

TO MY OLD SCHOOLMASTER

AN EPISTLE NOT AFTER THE MANNER OF HORACE

These lines were addressed to my worthy friend Joshua Coffin, teacher, historian, and antiquarian. He was one of the twelve persons who with William Lloyd Garrison formed the first anti-slavery society in New England.

OLD friend, kind friend! lightly down
    Drop time's snow-flakes on thy crown!
Never be thy shadow less,
Never fail thy cheerfulness;
Care, that kills the cat, may plough
Wrinkles in the miser's brow,
Deepen envy's spiteful frown,
Draw the mouths of bigots down,
Plague ambition's dream, and sit
Heavy on the hypocrite,
Haunt the rich man's door, and ride
In the gilded coach of pride; —
Let the fiend pass! — what can he
Find to do with such as thee?
Seldom comes that evil guest
Where the conscience lies at rest,
And brown health and quiet wit
Smiling on the threshold sit.

I, the urchin unto whom,
In that smoked and dingy room,
Where the district gave thee rule
O'er its ragged winter school,

TO MY OLD SCHOOLMASTER

Thou didst teach the mysteries
Of those weary A B C's, —
Where, to fill the every pause
Of thy wise and learned saws,
Through the cracked and crazy wall
Came the cradle-rock and squall,
And the goodman's voice, at strife
With his shrill and tipsy wife, —
Luring us by stories old,
With a comic unction told,
More than by the eloquence
Of terse birchen arguments
(Doubtful gain, I fear), to look
With complacence on a book! —
Where the genial pedagogue
Half forgot his rogues to flog,
Citing tale or apologue,
Wise and merry in its drift
As was Phædrus' twofold gift,
Had the little rebels known it,
Risum et prudentiam monet!
I, — the man of middle years,
In whose sable locks appears
Many a warning fleck of gray, —
Looking back to that far day,
And thy primal lessons, feel
Grateful smiles my lips unseal,
As, remembering thee, I blend
Olden teacher, present friend,
Wise with antiquarian search,
In the scrolls of State and Church:
Named on history's title-page,
Parish-clerk and justice sage;

For the ferule's wholesome awe
Wielding now the sword of law.

Threshing Time's neglected sheaves,
Gathering up the scattered leaves
Which the wrinkled sibyl cast
Careless from her as she passed, —
Twofold citizen art thou,
Freeman of the past and now.
He who bore thy name of old
Midway in the heavens did hold
Over Gibeon moon and sun;
Thou hast bidden them backward run
Of to-day the present ray
Flinging over yesterday!

Let the busy ones deride
What I deem of right thy pride:
Let the fools their treadmills grind,
Look not forward nor behind,
Shuffle in and wriggle out,
Veer with every breeze about,
Turning like a windmill sail,
Or a dog that seeks his tail;
Let them laugh to see thee fast
Tabernacled in the Past,
Working out with eye and lip
Riddles of old penmanship,
Patient as Belzoni there
Sorting out, with loving care,
Mummies of dead questions stripped
From their sevenfold manuscript!

Dabbling, in their noisy way,
In the puddles of to-day,
Little know they of that vast
Solemn ocean of the past,
On whose margin, wreck-bespread,
Thou art walking with the dead,
Questioning the stranded years,
Waking smiles by turns, and tears,
As thou callest up again
Shapes the dust has long o'erlain, —
Fair-haired woman, bearded man,
Cavalier and Puritan;
In an age whose eager view
Seeks but present things, and new,
Mad for party, sect and gold,
Teaching reverence for the old.

On that shore, with fowler's tact,
Coolly bagging fact on fact,
Naught amiss to thee can float,
Tale, or song, or anecdote;
Village gossip, centuries old,
Scandals by our grandams told,
What the pilgrim's table spread,
Where he lived, and whom he wed,
Long-drawn bill of wine and beer
For his ordination cheer,
Or the flip that wellnigh made
Glad his funeral cavalcade;
Weary prose, and poet's lines,
Flavored by their age, like wines,
Eulogistic of some quaint,
Doubtful, Puritanic saint:

Lays that quickened husking jigs,
Jests that shook grave periwigs,
When the parson had his jokes
And his glass, like other folks;
Sermons that, for mortal hours,
Taxed our fathers' vital powers,
As the long nineteenthlies poured
Downward from the sounding-board,
And, for fire of Pentecost,
Touched their beards December's frost.

Time is hastening on, and we
What our fathers are shall be, —
Shadow-shapes of memory!
Joined to that vast multitude
Where the great are but the good,
And the mind of strength shall prove
Weaker than the heart of love;
Pride of graybeard wisdom less
Than the infant's guilelessness,
And his song of sorrow more
Than the crown the Psalmist wore!
Who shall then, with pious zeal,
At our moss-grown thresholds kneel,
From a stained and stony page
Reading to a careless age,
With a patient eye like thine,
Prosing tale and limping line,
Names and words the hoary rime
Of the Past has made sublime?
Who shall work for us as well
The antiquarian's miracle?

Who to seeming life recall
Teacher grave and pupil small?
Who shall give to thee and me
Freeholds in futurity?

Well, whatever lot be mine,
Long and happy days be thine,
Ere thy full and honored age
Dates of time its latest page!
Squire for master, State for school,
Wisely lenient, live and rule;
Over grown-up knave and rogue
Play the watchful pedagogue;
Or, while pleasure smiles on duty,
At the call of youth and beauty,
Speak for them the spell of law
Which shall bar and bolt withdraw,
And the flaming sword remove
From the Paradise of Love.
Still, with undimmed eyesight, pore
Ancient tome and record o'er;
Still thy week-day lyrics croon,
Pitch in church the Sunday tune,
Showing something, in thy part,
Of the old Puritanic art,
Singer after Sternhold's heart!
In thy pew, for many a year,
Homilies from Oldbug hear,
Who to wit like that of South,
And the Syrian's golden mouth,
Doth the homely pathos add
Which the pilgrim preachers had;

Breaking, like a child at play,
Gilded idols of the day,
Cant of knave and pomp of fool
Tossing with his ridicule,
Yet, in earnest or in jest,
Ever keeping truth abreast.
And, when thou art called, at last,
To thy townsmen of the past,
Not as stranger shalt thou come;
Thou shalt find thyself at home
With the little and the big,
Woollen cap and periwig,
Madam in her high-laced ruff,
Goody in her home-made stuff, —
Wise and simple, rich and poor,
Thou hast known them all before!

IN SCHOOL-DAYS

STILL sits the school-house by the road
   A ragged beggar sleeping;
Around it still the sumachs grow,
   And blackberry-vines are creeping.

Within, the master's desk is seen,
   Deep scarred by raps official;
The warping floor, the battered seats,
   The jack-knife's carved initial;

The charcoal frescos on its wall;
   Its door's worn sill, betraying
The feet that, creeping slow to school,
   Went storming out to playing!

IN SCHOOL-DAYS

Long years ago a winter sun
  Shone over it at setting;
Lit up its western window-panes,
  And low eaves' icy fretting.

It touched the tangled golden curls,
  And brown eyes full of grieving,
Of one who still her steps delayed
  When all the school were leaving.

For near her stood the little boy
  Her childish favor singled:
His cap pulled low upon a face
  Where pride and shame were mingled.

Pushing with restless feet the snow
  To right and left, he lingered; —
As restlessly her tiny hands
  The blue-checked apron fingered.

He saw her lift her eyes; he felt
  The soft hand's light caressing,
And heard the tremble of her voice,
  As if a fault confessing.

"I 'm sorry that I spelt the word:
  I hate to go above you,
Because," — the brown eyes lower fell, —
  "Because, you see, I love you!"

Still memory to a gray-haired man
  That sweet child-face is showing.

Dear girl! the grasses on her grave
   Have forty years been growing!

He lives to learn, in life's hard school
   How few who pass above him
Lament their triumph and his loss,
   Like her,— because they love him.

MY PLAYMATE

THE pines were dark on Ramoth hill
   Their song was soft and low;
The blossoms in the sweet May wind
   Were falling like the snow.

The blossoms drifted at our feet,
   The orchard birds sang clear;
The sweetest and the saddest day
   It seemed of all the year.

For, more to me than birds or flowers,
   My playmate left her home,
And took with her the laughing spring,
   The music and the bloom.

She kissed the lips of kith and kin,
   She laid her hand in mine:
What more could ask the bashful boy
   Who fed her father's kine?

She left us in the bloom of May:
   The constant years told o'er

Their seasons with as sweet May morns,
   But she came back no more.

I walk, with noiseless feet, the round
   Of uneventful years ;
Still o'er and o'er I sow the spring
   And reap the autumn ears.

She lives where all the golden year
   Her summer roses blow ;
The dusky children of the sun
   Before her come and go.

There haply with her jewelled hands
   She smooths her silken gown, —
No more the homespun lap wherein
   I shook the walnuts down.

The wild grapes wait us by the brook,
   The brown nuts on the hill,
And still the May-day flowers make sweet
   The woods of Follymill.

The lilies blossom in the pond,
   The bird builds in the tree,
The dark pines sing on Ramoth hill
   The slow song of the sea.

I wonder if she thinks of them,
   And how the old time seems, —
If ever the pines of Ramoth wood
   Are sounding in her dreams.

I see her face, I hear her voice;
   Does she remember mine?
And what to her is now the boy
   Who fed her father's kine?

What cares she that the orioles build
   For other eyes than ours, —
That other hands with nuts are filled,
   And other laps with flowers?

O playmate in the golden time!
   Our mossy seat is green,
Its fringing violets blossom yet,
   The old trees o'er it lean.

The winds so sweet with birch and fern
   A sweeter memory blow;
And there in spring the veeries sing
   The song of long ago.

And still the pines of Ramoth wood
   Are moaning like the sea, —
The moaning of the sea of change
   Between myself and thee!

MEMORIES

"It was not without thought and deliberation," Whittier's biographer writes, "that in 1888 he directed this poem to be placed at the head of his Poems Subjective and Reminiscent. He had never before publicly acknowledged how much of his heart was wrapped up in this delightful play of poetic fancy. The poem was written in 1841, and although the romance it embalms lies far back of this date, possibly there is a heart still beating which fully understands its meaning. The biographer can do no more than make this suggestion, which has the sanction of the poet's explicit word. To a friend who told him that *Memories* was her favorite poem, he said, 'I love it too; but I hardly knew whether to publish it, it was so personal and near my heart.'"

A BEAUTIFUL and happy girl,
    With step as light as summer air,
Eyes glad with smiles, and brow of pearl,
Shadowed by many a careless curl
    Of unconfined and flowing hair;
A seeming child in everything,
    Save thoughtful brow and ripening charms,
As Nature wears the smile of Spring
    When sinking into Summer's arms.

A mind rejoicing in the light
    Which melted through its graceful bower,
Leaf after leaf, dew-moist and bright,
And stainless in its holy white,
    Unfolding like a morning flower:
A heart, which, like a fine-toned lute,
    With every breath of feeling woke,
And, even when the tongue was mute,
    From eye and lip in music spoke.

How thrills once more the lengthening chain
    Of memory, at the thought of thee!
Old hopes which long in dust have lain,
Old dreams, come thronging back again,
    And boyhood lives again in me;

I feel its glow upon my cheek,
  Its fulness of the heart is mine,
As when I leaned to hear thee speak,
  Or raised my doubtful eye to thine.

I hear again thy low replies,
  I feel thy arm within my own,
And timidly again uprise
The fringèd lids of hazel eyes,
  With soft brown tresses overblown.
Ah! memories of sweet summer eves,
  Of moonlit wave and willowy way,
Of stars and flowers, and dewy leaves,
  And smiles and tones more dear than they!

Ere this, thy quiet eye hath smiled
  My picture of thy youth to see,
When, half a woman, half a child,
Thy very artlessness beguiled,
  And folly's self seemed wise in thee;
I too can smile, when o'er that hour
  The lights of memory backward stream,
Yet feel the while that manhood's power
  Is vainer than my boyhood's dream.

Years have passed on, and left their trace,
  Of graver care and deeper thought;
And unto me the calm, cold face
Of manhood, and to thee the grace
  Of woman's pensive beauty brought.
More wide, perchance, for blame than praise,
  The school-boy's humble name has flown;

Thine, in the green and quiet ways
   Of unobtrusive goodness known.

And wider yet in thought and deed
   Diverge our pathways, one in youth;
Thine the Genevan's sternest creed,
While answers to my spirit's need
   The Derby dalesman's simple truth.
For thee, the priestly rite and prayer,
   And holy day, and solemn psalm;
For me, the silent reverence where
   My brethren gather, slow and calm.

Yet hath thy spirit left on me
   An impress Time has worn not out,
And something of myself in thee,
A shadow from the past, I see,
   Lingering, even yet, thy way about;
Not wholly can the heart unlearn
   That lesson of its better hours,
Not yet has Time's dull footstep worn
   To common dust that path of flowers.

Thus, while at times before our eyes
   The shadows melt, and fall apart,
And, smiling through them, round us lies
The warm light of our morning skies,—
   The Indian Summer of the heart!
In secret sympathies of mind,
   In founts of feeling which retain
Their pure, fresh flow, we yet may find
   Our early dreams not wholly vain!

Tangles his wings of fire in the trees,
   Setting, as then, over Fernside farm.

I mind me how with a lover's care
   From my Sunday coat
I brushed off the burrs, and smoothed my hair,
   And cooled at the brookside my brow and throat.

Since we parted, a month had passed, —
   To love, a year;
Down through the beeches I looked at last
   On the little red gate and the well-sweep near.

I can see it all now, — the slantwise rain
   Of light through the leaves,
The sundown's blaze on her window-pane,
   The bloom of her roses under the eaves.

Just the same as a month before, —
   The house and the trees,
The barn's brown gable, the vine by the door, —
   Nothing changed but the hives of bees.

Before them, under the garden wall,
   Forward and back,
Went drearily singing the chore-girl small,
   Draping each hive with a shred of black.

Trembling, I listened: the summer sun
   Had the chill of snow;
For I knew she was telling the bees of one
   Gone on the journey we all must go!

How, at their mention, memory turns
   Her pages old and pleasant!

The gray sky wears again its gold
   And purple of adorning,
And manhood's noonday shadows hold
   The dews of boyhood's morning.

The dews that washed the dust and soil
   From off the wings of pleasure,
The sky, that flecked the ground of toil
   With golden threads of leisure.

I call to mind the summer day,
   The early harvest mowing,
The sky with sun and clouds at play,
   And flowers with breezes blowing.

I hear the blackbird in the corn,
   The locust in the haying;
And, like the fabled hunter's horn,
   Old tunes my heart is playing.

How oft that day, with fond delay,
   I sought the maple's shadow,
And sang with Burns the hours away,
   Forgetful of the meadow!

Bees hummed, birds twittered, overhead
   I heard the squirrels leaping,
The good dog listened while I read,
   And wagged his tail in keeping.

I watched him while in sportive mood
  I read " *The Twa Dogs*' " story,
And half believed he understood
  The poet's allegory.

Sweet day, sweet songs! The golden hours
  Grew brighter for that singing,
From brook and bird and meadow flowers
  A dearer welcome bringing.

New light on home-seen Nature beamed,
  New glory over Woman;
And daily life and duty seemed
  No longer poor and common.

I woke to find the simple truth
  Of fact and feeling better
Than all the dreams that held my youth
  A still repining debtor:

That Nature gives her handmaid, Art,
  The themes of sweet discoursing;
The tender idyls of the heart
  In every tongue rehearsing.

Why dream of lands of gold and pearl,
  Of loving knight and lady,
When farmer boy and barefoot girl
  Were wandering there already?

I saw through all familiar things
  The romance underlying;

The joys and griefs that plume the wings
  Of Fancy skyward flying.

I saw the same blithe day return,
  The same sweet fall of even,
That rose on wooded Craigie-burn,
  And sank on crystal Devon.

I matched with Scotland's heathery hills
  The sweetbrier and the clover;
With Ayr and Doon, my native rills,
  Their wood hymns chanting over.

O'er rank and pomp, as he had seen,
  I saw the Man uprising;
No longer common or unclean,
  The child of God's baptizing!

With clearer eyes I saw the worth
  Of life among the lowly;
The Bible at his Cotter's hearth
  Had made my own more holy.

And if at times an evil strain,
  To lawless love appealing,
Broke in upon the sweet refrain
  Of pure and healthful feeling,

It died upon the eye and ear,
  No inward answer gaining;
No heart had I to see or hear
  The discord and the staining.

Let those who never erred forget
  His worth, in vain bewailings;
Sweet Soul of Song! I own my debt
  Uncancelled by his failings!

Lament who will the ribald line
  Which tells his lapse from duty,
How kissed the maddening lips of wine
  Or wanton ones of beauty;

But think, while falls that shade between
  The erring one and Heaven,
That he who loved like Magdalen,
  Like her may be forgiven.

Not his the song whose thunderous chime
  Eternal echoes render;
The mournful Tuscan's haunted rhyme,
  And Milton's starry splendor!

But who his human heart has laid
  To Nature's bosom nearer?
Who sweetened toil like him, or paid
  To love a tribute dearer?

Through all his tuneful art, how strong
  The human feeling gushes!
The very moonlight of his song
  Is warm with smiles and blushes!

Give lettered pomp to teeth of Time,
  So "Bonnie Doon" but tarry;
Blot out the Epic's stately rhyme,
  But spare his Highland Mary!

TO MY SISTER

WITH A COPY OF "THE SUPERNATURALISM OF NEW ENGLAND"

The work referred to was a series of papers under this title, contributed to the *Democratic Review* and afterward collected into a volume, in which I noted some of the superstitions and folklore prevalent in New England. The volume has not been kept in print, but most of its contents are distributed in my *Literary Recreations and Miscellanies* [now scattered in volumes v. and vi. of the Riverside edition].

DEAR Sister! while the wise and sage
   Turn coldly from my playful page,
And count it strange that ripened age
   Should stoop to boyhood's folly;
I know that thou wilt judge aright
Of all which makes the heart more light,
Or lends one star-gleam to the night
   Of clouded Melancholy.

Away with weary cares and themes
Swing wide the moonlit gate of dreams!
Leave free once more the land which teems
   With wonders and romances!
Where thou, with clear discerning eyes,
Shalt rightly read the truth which lies
Beneath the quaintly masking guise
   Of wild and wizard fancies.

Lo! once again our feet we set
On still green wood-paths, twilight wet,

By lonely brooks, whose waters fret
    The roots of spectral beeches;
Again the hearth fire glimmers o'er
Home's whitewashed wall and painted floor,
And young eyes widening to the lore
    Of faery-folks and witches.

Dear heart! the legend is not vain
Which lights that holy hearth again,
And calling back from care and pain,
    And death's funereal sadness,
Draws round its old familiar blaze
The clustering groups of happier days,
And lends to sober manhood's gaze
    A glimpse of childish gladness.

And, knowing how my life hath been
A weary work of tongue and pen,
A long, harsh strife with strong-willed men,
    Thou wilt not chide my turning
To con, at times, an idle rhyme,
To pluck a flower from childhood's clime,
Or listen, at Life's noonday chime,
    For the sweet bells of Morning!

ICHABOD

This poem was the outcome of the surprise and grief and forecast of evil consequences which I felt on reading the seventh of March speech of Daniel Webster in support of the "compromise," and the Fugitive Slave Law. No partisan or personal enmity dictated it. On the contrary my admiration of the splendid personality and intellectual power of the great Senator was never stronger than when I laid down his speech, and, in one of the saddest moments of my life, penned my protest. I saw, as I wrote, with painful clearness its sure results, — the Slave Power arrogant and defiant, strengthened and encouraged to carry out its scheme for the extension of its baleful system, or the dissolution of the Union, the guaranties of personal liberty in the free States broken down, and the whole country made the hunting-ground of slave-catchers. In the horror of such a vision, so soon fearfully fulfilled, if one spoke at all, he could only speak in tones of stern and sorrowful rebuke.

But death softens all resentments, and the consciousness of a common inheritance of frailty and weakness modifies the severity of judgment. Years after, in *The Lost Occasion*, I gave utterance to an almost universal regret that the great statesman did not live to see the flag which he loved trampled under the feet of Slavery, and, in view of this desecration, make his last days glorious in defence of "Liberty and Union, one and inseparable."

SO fallen! so lost! the light withdrawn
    Which once he wore!
The glory from his gray hairs gone
    Forevermore!

Revile him not, the Tempter hath
    A snare for all;
And pitying tears, not scorn and wrath,
    Befit his fall!

Oh, dumb be passion's stormy rage,
    When he who might
Have lighted up and led his age,
    Falls back in night.

Scorn! would the angels laugh, to mark
    A bright soul driven,
Fiend-goaded, down the endless dark,
    From hope and heaven!

Let not the land once proud of him
    Insult him now,
Nor brand with deeper shame his dim,
    Dishonored brow.

But let its humbled sons, instead,
    From sea to lake,
A long lament, as for the dead,
    In sadness make.

Of all we loved and honored, naught
    Save power remains;
A fallen angel's pride of thought,
    Still strong in chains.

All else is gone; from those great eyes
    The soul has fled:
When faith is lost, when honor dies,
    The man is dead!

Then, pay the reverence of old days
    To his dead fame;
Walk backward, with averted gaze,
    And hide the shame!

THE LOST OCCASION

SOME die too late and some too soon,
  At early morning, heat of noon,
Or the chill evening twilight. Thou,
Whom the rich heavens did so endow
With eyes of power and Jove's own brow,
With all the massive strength that fills
Thy home-horizon's granite hills,
With rarest gifts of heart and head
From manliest stock inherited,
New England's stateliest type of man,
In port and speech Olympian;
Whom no one met, at first, but took
A second awed and wondering look
(As turned, perchance, the eyes of Greece
On Phidias' unveiled masterpiece);
Whose words in simplest homespun clad,
The Saxon strength of Cædmon's had,
With power reserved at need to reach
The Roman forum's loftiest speech,
Sweet with persuasion, eloquent
In passion, cool in argument,
Or, ponderous, falling on thy foes
As fell the Norse god's hammer blows,
Crushing as if with Talus' flail
Through Error's logic-woven mail,
And failing only when they tried
The adamant of the righteous side, —
Thou, foiled in aim and hope, bereaved
Of old friends, by the new deceived,

THE LOST OCCASION

Too soon for us, too soon for thee,
Beside thy lonely Northern sea,
Where long and low the marsh-lands spread,
Laid wearily down thy august head.

Thou shouldst have lived to feel below
Thy feet Disunion's fierce upthrow;
The late-sprung mine that underlaid
Thy sad concessions vainly made.
Thou shouldst have seen from Sumter's wall
The star-flag of the Union fall,
And armed rebellion pressing on
The broken lines of Washington!
No stronger voice than thine had then
Called out the utmost might of men,
To make the Union's charter free
And strengthen law by liberty.
How had that stern arbitrament
To thy gray age youth's vigor lent,
Shaming ambition's paltry prize
Before thy disillusioned eyes;
Breaking the spell about thee wound
Like the green withes that Samson bound;
Redeeming in one effort grand,
Thyself and thy imperilled land!
Ah, cruel fate, that closed to thee,
O sleeper by the Northern sea,
The gates of opportunity!
God fills the gaps of human need,
Each crisis brings its word and deed.
Wise men and strong we did not lack;
But still, with memory turning back,

THE LOST OCCASION

In the dark hours we thought of thee,
And thy lone grave beside the sea.

Above that grave the east winds blow,
And from the marsh-lands drifting slow
The sea-fog comes, with evermore
The wave-wash of a lonely shore,
And sea-bird's melancholy cry,
As Nature fain would typify
The sadness of a closing scene,
The loss of that which should have been.
But, where thy native mountains bare
Their foreheads to diviner air,
Fit emblem of enduring fame,
One lofty summit keeps thy name.
For thee the cosmic forces did
The rearing of that pyramid,
The prescient ages shaping with
Fire, flood, and frost thy monolith.
Sunrise and sunset lay thereon
With hands of light their benison,
The stars of midnight pause to set
Their jewels in its coronet.
And evermore that mountain mass
Seems climbing from the shadowy pass
To light, as if to manifest
Thy nobler self, thy life at best!

THE QUAKER OF THE OLDEN TIME

THE Quaker of the olden time!
  How calm and firm and true,
Unspotted by its wrong and crime,
  He walked the dark earth through.
The lust of power, the love of gain,
  The thousand lures of sin
Around him, had no power to stain
  The purity within.

With that deep insight which detects
  All great things in the small,
And knows how each man's life affects
  The spiritual life of all,
He walked by faith and not by sight,
  By love and not by law;
The presence of the wrong or right
  He rather felt than saw.

He felt that wrong with wrong partakes,
  That nothing stands alone,
That whoso gives the motive, makes
  His brother's sin his own.
And, pausing not for doubtful choice
  Of evils great or small,
He listened to that inward voice
  Which called away from all.

O Spirit of that early day,
  So pure and strong and true,

Be with us in the narrow way
  Our faithful fathers knew.
Give strength the evil to forsake,
  The cross of Truth to bear,
And love and reverent fear to make
  Our daily lives a prayer!

THE MEETING

The two speakers in the meeting referred to in this poem were Avis Keene, whose very presence was a benediction, a woman lovely in spirit and person, whose words seemed a message of love and tender concern to her hearers; and Sibyl Jones, whose inspired eloquence and rare spirituality impressed all who knew her. In obedience to her apprehended duty she made visits of Christian love to various parts of Europe, and to the West Coast of Africa and Palestine.

THE elder folk shook hands at last,
  Down seat by seat the signal passed.
To simple ways like ours unused,
Half solemnized and half amused,
With long-drawn breath and shrug, my guest
His sense of glad relief expressed.
Outside, the hills lay warm in sun;
The cattle in the meadow-run
Stood half-leg deep; a single bird
The green repose above us stirred.
"What part or lot have you," he said,
"In these dull rites of drowsy-head?
Is silence worship? Seek it where
It soothes with dreams the summer air,
Not in this close and rude-benched hall.

But where soft lights and shadows fall,
And all the slow, sleep-walking hours
Glide soundless over grass and flowers!
From time and place and form apart,
Its holy ground the human heart,
Nor ritual-bound nor templeward
Walks the free spirit of the Lord!
Our common Master did not pen
His followers up from other men;
His service liberty indeed,
He built no church, He framed no creed;
But while the saintly Pharisee
Made broader his phylactery,
As from the synagogue was seen
The dusty-sandalled Nazarene
Through ripening cornfields lead the way
Upon the awful Sabbath day,
His sermons were the healthful talk
That shorter made the mountain-walk,
His wayside texts were flowers and birds,
Where mingled with His gracious words
The rustle of the tamarisk-tree
And ripple-wash of Galilee."

" Thy words are well, O friend," I said;
" Unmeasured and unlimited,
With noiseless slide of stone to stone,
The mystic Church of God has grown.
Invisible and silent stands
The temple never made with hands,
Unheard the voices still and small
Of its unseen confessional.

THE MEETING

He needs no special place of prayer
Whose hearing ear is everywhere;
He brings not back the childish days
That ringed the earth with stones of praise,
Roofed Karnak's hall of gods, and laid
The plinths of Philæ's colonnade.
Still less He owns the selfish good
And sickly growth of solitude, —
The worthless grace that, out of sight,
Flowers in the desert anchorite;
Dissevered from the suffering whole,
Love hath no power to save a soul.
Not out of Self, the origin
And native air and soil of sin,
The living waters spring and flow,
The trees with leaves of healing grow.

Dream not, O friend, because I seek
This quiet shelter twice a week,
I better deem its pine-laid floor
Than breezy hill or sea-sung shore;
But nature is not solitude:
She crowds us with her thronging wood;
Her many hands reach out to us,
Her many tongues are garrulous;
Perpetual riddles of surprise
She offers to our ears and eyes;
She will not leave our senses still,
But drags them captive at her will:
And, making earth too great for heaven,
She hides the Giver in the given.

THE MEETING

" And so I find it well to come
For deeper rest to this still room,
For here the habit of the soul
Feels less the outer world's control;
The strength of mutual purpose pleads
More earnestly our common needs;
And from the silence multiplied
By these still forms on either side,
The world that time and sense have known
Falls off and leaves us God alone.

" Yet rarely through the charmed repose
Unmixed the stream of motive flows,
A flavor of its many springs,
The tints of earth and sky it brings;
In the still waters needs must be
Some shade of human sympathy;
And here, in its accustomed place,
I look on memory's dearest face;
The blind by-sitter guesseth not
What shadow haunts that vacant spot;
No eyes save mine alone can see
The love wherewith it welcomes me!
And still, with those alone my kin,
In doubt and weakness, want and sin,
I bow my head, my heart I bare,
As when that face was living there,
And strive (too oft, alas! in vain)
The peace of simple trust to gain,
Fold fancy's restless wings, and lay
The idols of my heart away.

THE MEETING

Welcome the silence all unbroken,
Nor less the words of fitness spoken, —
Such golden words as hers for whom
Our autumn flowers have just made room;
Whose hopeful utterance through and through
The freshness of the morning blew;
Who loved not less the earth that light
Fell on it from the heavens in sight,
But saw in all fair forms more fair
The Eternal beauty mirrored there.
Whose eighty years but added grace
And saintlier meaning to her face, —
The look of one who bore away
Glad tidings from the hills of day,
While all our hearts went forth to meet
The coming of her beautiful feet!
Or haply hers, whose pilgrim tread
Is in the paths where Jesus led;
Who dreams her childhood's sabbath dream
By Jordan's willow-shaded stream,
And, of the hymns of hope and faith,
Sung by the monks of Nazareth,
Hears pious echoes, in the call
To prayer, from Moslem minarets fall,
Repeating where His works were wrought
The lesson that her Master taught
Of whom an elder Sibyl gave
The prophecies of Cumæ's cave!

I ask no organ's soulless breath
To drone the themes of life and death.

THE MEETING

No altar candle-lit by day,
No ornate wordsman's rhetoric-play,
No cool philosophy to teach
Its bland audacities of speech
To double-tasked idolaters
Themselves their gods and worshippers,
No pulpit hammered by the fist
Of loud-asserting dogmatist,
Who borrows for the Hand of love
The smoking thunderbolts of Jove.
I know how well the fathers taught,
What work the later schoolmen wrought;
I reverence old-time faith and men,
But God is near us now as then;
His force of love is still unspent,
His hate of sin as imminent;
And still the measure of our needs
Outgrows the cramping bounds of creeds;
The manna gathered yesterday
Already savors of decay;
Doubts to the world's child-heart unknown
Question us now from star and stone;
Too little or too much we know,
And sight is swift and faith is slow;
The power is lost to self-deceive
With shallow forms of make-believe.
We walk at high noon, and the bells
Call to a thousand oracles,
But the sound deafens, and the light
Is stronger than our dazzled sight;
The letters of the sacred Book
Glimmer and swim beneath our look:

THE MEETING

Still struggles in the Age's breast
With deepening agony of quest
The old entreaty: 'Art thou He,
Or look we for the Christ to be?'

God should be most where man is least:
So, where is neither church nor priest,
And never rag of form or creed
To clothe the nakedness of need, —
Where farmer-folk in silence meet, —
I turn my bell-unsummoned feet;
I lay the critic's glass aside,
I tread upon my lettered pride,
And, lowest-seated, testify
To the oneness of humanity;
Confess the universal want,
And share whatever Heaven may grant.
He findeth not who seeks his own,
The soul is lost that 's saved alone.
Not on one favored forehead fell
Of old the fire-tongued miracle,
But flamed o'er all the thronging host
The baptism of the Holy Ghost;
Heart answers heart: in one desire
The blending lines of prayer aspire;
Where, in my name, meet two or three,'
Our Lord hath said, 'I there will be!'

So sometimes comes to soul and sense
The feeling which is evidence
That very near about us lies
The realm of spiritual mysteries.

The sphere of the supernal powers
Impinges on this world of ours.
The low and dark horizon lifts,
To light the scenic terror shifts;
The breath of a diviner air
Blows down the answer of a prayer:
That all our sorrow, pain, and doubt
A great compassion clasps about,
And law and goodness, love and force
Are wedded fast beyond divorce.
Then duty leaves to love its task,
The beggar Self forgets to ask;
With smile of trust and folded hands,
The passive soul in waiting stands
To feel, as flowers the sun and dew,
The One true Life its own renew.

"So to the calmly gathered thought
The innermost of truth is taught,
The mystery dimly understood,
That love of God is love of good,
And, chiefly, its divinest trace
In Him of Nazareth's holy face;
That to be saved is only this, —
Salvation from our selfishness,
From more than elemental fire,
The soul's unsanctified desire,
From sin itself, and not the pain
That warns us of its chafing chain;
That worship's deeper meaning lies
In mercy, and not sacrifice,
Not proud humilities of sense

And posturing of penitence,
But love's unforced obedience;
That Book and Church and Day are given
For man, not God, — for earth, not heaven, —
The blessed means to holiest ends,
Not masters, but benignant friends;
That the dear Christ dwells not afar,
The king of some remoter star,
Listening, at times, with flattered ear
To homage wrung from selfish fear,
But here, amidst the poor and blind,
The bound and suffering of our kind,
In works we do, in prayers we pray,
Life of our life, He lives to-day."

HAMPTON BEACH

THE sunlight glitters keen and bright,
    Where, miles away,
Lies stretching to my dazzled sight
A luminous belt, a misty light,
Beyond the dark pine bluffs and wastes of sandy
    gray.

The tremulous shadow of the Sea!
    Against its ground
Of silvery light, rock, hill, and tree,
Still as a picture, clear and free,
With varying outline mark the coast for miles
    around.

HAMPTON BEACH

    Our seaward way,
On — on — we tread with loose-flung rein
Through dark-green fields and blossoming grain,
Where the wild brier-rose skirts the lane,
And bends above our heads the flowering locust
    spray.

    Ha! like a kind hand on my brow
        Comes this fresh breeze,
Cooling its dull and feverish glow,
While through my being seems to flow
The breath of a new life, the healing of the seas!

    Now rest we, where this grassy mound
        His feet hath set
In the great waters, which have bound
His granite ankles greenly round
With long and tangled moss, and weeds with cool
    spray wet.

    Good-by to Pain and Care! I take
        Mine ease to-day:
Here where these sunny waters break,
And ripples this keen breeze, I shake
All burdens from the heart, all weary thoughts
    away.

    I draw a freer breath, I seem
        Like all I see —
Waves in the sun, the white-winged gleam
Of sea-birds in the slanting beam,
And far-off sails which flit before the south-wind
    free.

HAMPTON BEACH

So when Time's veil shall fall asunder,
  The soul may know
No fearful change, nor sudden wonder,
Nor sink the weight of mystery under,
But with the upward rise, and with the vastness
  grow.

And all we shrink from now may seem
  No new revealing;
Familiar as our childhood's stream,
Or pleasant memory of a dream
The loved and cherished Past upon the new life
  stealing.

Serene and mild the untried light
  May have its dawning;
And, as in summer's northern night
The evening and the dawn unite,
The sunset hues of Time blend with the soul's
  new morning.

I sit alone; in foam and spray
  Wave after wave
Breaks on the rocks which, stern and gray,
Shoulder the broken tide away,
Or murmurs hoarse and strong through mossy
  cleft and cave.

What heed I of the dusty land
  And noisy town?
I see the mighty deep expand

From its white line of glimmering sand
To where the blue of heaven on bluer waves shuts
   down!

In listless quietude of mind,
    I yield to all
The change of cloud and wave and wind;
And passive on the flood reclined,
I wander with the waves, and with them rise and
   fall.

But look, thou dreamer! wave and shore
    In shadow lie;
The night-wind warns me back once more
To where, my native hill-tops o'er,
Bends like an arch of fire the glowing sunset sky.

So then, beach, bluff, and wave, farewell!
    I bear with me
No token stone nor glittering shell,
But long and oft shall Memory tell
Of this brief thoughtful hour of musing by the
   Sea.

A SEA DREAM

WE saw the slow tides go and come,
    The curving surf-lines lightly drawn,
The gray rocks touched with tender bloom
    Beneath the fresh-blown rose of dawn.

A SEA DREAM

We saw in richer sunsets lost
  The sombre pomp of showery noons;
And signalled spectral sails that crossed
  The weird, low light of rising moons.

On stormy eves from cliff and head
  We saw the white spray tossed and spurned;
While over all, in gold and red,
  Its face of fire the lighthouse turned.

The rail-car brought its daily crowds,
  Half curious, half indifferent,
Like passing sails or floating clouds,
  We saw them as they came and went.

But, one calm morning, as we lay
  And watched the mirage-lifted wall
Of coast, across the dreamy bay,
  And heard afar the curlew call,

And nearer voices, wild or tame,
  Of airy flock and childish throng,
Up from the water's edge there came
  Faint snatches of familiar song.

Careless we heard the singer's choice
  Of old and common airs; at last
The tender pathos of his voice
  In one low chanson held us fast.

A song that mingled joy and pain,
  And memories old and sadly sweet;

A SEA DREAM

While, timing to its minor strain,
  The waves in lapsing cadence beat.

The waves are glad in breeze and sun;
  The rocks are fringed with foam;
I walk once more a haunted shore,
  A stranger, yet at home,
  A land of dreams I roam.

Is this the wind, the soft sea-wind
  That stirred thy locks of brown?
Are these the rocks whose mosses knew
  The trail of thy light gown,
  Where boy and girl sat down?

I see the gray fort's broken wall,
  The boats that rock below;
And, out at sea, the passing sails
  We saw so long ago
  Rose-red in morning's glow.

The freshness of the early time
  On every breeze is blown;
As glad the sea, as blue the sky, —
  The change is ours alone;
  The saddest is my own.

A stranger now, a world-worn man,
  Is he who bears my name;
But thou, methinks, whose mortal life
  Immortal youth became,
  Art evermore the same.

A SEA DREAM

Thou art not here, thou art not there,
  Thy place I cannot see;
I only know that where thou art
  The blessed angels be,
  And heaven is glad for thee.

Forgive me if the evil years
  Have left on me their sign;
Wash out, O soul so beautiful,
  The many stains of mine
  In tears of love divine!

I could not look on thee and live,
  If thou wert by my side;
The vision of a shining one,
  The white and heavenly bride,
  Is well to me denied.

But turn to me thy dear girl-face
  Without the angel's crown,
The wedded roses of thy lips,
  Thy loose hair rippling down
  In waves of golden brown.

Look forth once more through space and time,
  And let thy sweet shade fall
In tenderest grace of soul and form
  On memory's frescoed wall,
  A shadow, and yet all!

Draw near, more near, forever dear!
  Where'er I rest or roam,

Or in the city's crowded streets,
  Or by the blown sea foam,
The thought of thee is home!

At breakfast hour the singer read
  The city news, with comment wise,
Like one who felt the pulse of trade
  Beneath his finger fall and rise.

His look, his air, his curt speech, told
  The man of action, not of books,
To whom the corners made in gold
  And stocks were more than seaside nooks

Of life beneath the life confessed
  His song had hinted unawares;
Of flowers in traffic's ledgers pressed,
  Of human hearts in bulls and bears.

But eyes in vain were turned to watch
  That face so hard and shrewd and strong
And ears in vain grew sharp to catch
  The meaning of that morning song.

In vain some sweet-voiced querist sought
  To sound him, leaving as she came;
Her baited album only caught
  A common, unromantic name.

No word betrayed the mystery fine,
  That trembled on the singer's tongue;
He came and went, and left no sign
  Behind him save the song he sung.

SUMMER BY THE LAKESIDE

LAKE WINNIPESAUKEE

I. NOON

WHITE clouds, whose shadows haunt the deep
Light mists, whose soft embraces keep
The sunshine on the hills asleep!

O isles of calm! O dark, still wood!
And stiller skies that overbrood
Your rest with deeper quietude!

O shapes and hues, dim beckoning, through
Yon mountain gaps, my longing view
Beyond the purple and the blue,

To stiller sea and greener land,
And softer lights and airs more bland,
And skies, — the hollow of God's hand!

Transfused through you, O mountain friends!
With mine your solemn spirit blends,
And life no more hath separate ends.

I read each misty mountain sign,
I know the voice of wave and pine,
And I am yours, and ye are mine.

Life's burdens fall, its discords cease,
I lapse into the glad release
Of Nature's own exceeding peace.

O welcome calm of heart and mind!
As falls yon fir-tree's loosened rind
To leave a tenderer growth behind,

So fall the weary years away;
A child again, my head I lay
Upon the lap of this sweet day.

This western wind hath Lethean powers,
Yon noonday cloud nepenthe showers,
The lake is white with lotus-flowers!

Even Duty's voice is faint and low,
And slumberous Conscience, waking slow
Forgets her blotted scroll to show.

The Shadow which pursues us all,
Whose ever-nearing steps appall,
Whose voice we hear behind us call, —

That Shadow blends with mountain gray,
It speaks but what the light waves say, —
Death walks apart from Fear to-day!

Rocked on her breast, these pines and I
Alike on Nature's love rely ;
And equal seems to live or die.

Assured that He whose presence fills
With light the spaces of these hills
No evil to His creatures wills.

The simple faith remains, that He
Will do, whatever that may be,
The best alike for man and tree.

What mosses over one shall grow,
What light and life the other know,
Unanxious, leaving Him to show.

II. EVENING

Yon mountain's side is black with night,
 While, broad-orbed, o'er its gleaming crown
The moon, slow-rounding into sight,
 On the hushed inland sea looks down.

How start to light the clustering isles,
 Each silver-hemmed! How sharply show
The shadows of their rocky piles,
 And tree-tops in the wave below!

How far and strange the mountains seem,
 Dim-looming through the pale, still light!
The vague, vast grouping of a dream,
 They stretch into the solemn night.

Beneath, lake, wood, and peopled vale,
 Hushed by that presence grand and grave,
Are silent, save the cricket's wail,
 And low response of leaf and wave.

Fair scenes! whereto the Day and Night
 Make rival love, I leave ye soon,
What time before the eastern light
 The pale ghost of the setting moon

Shall hide behind yon rocky spines,
  And the young archer, Morn, shall break
His arrows on the mountain pines,
  And, golden-sandalled, walk the lake!

Farewell! around this smiling bay
  Gay-hearted Health, and Life in bloom,
With lighter steps than mine, may stray
  In radiant summers yet to come.

But none shall more regretful leave
  These waters and these hills than I:
Or, distant, fonder dream how eve
  Or dawn is painting wave and sky;

How rising moons shine sad and mild
  On wooded isle and silvering bay;
Or setting suns beyond the piled
  And purple mountains lead the day;

Nor laughing girl, nor bearding boy,
  Nor full-pulsed manhood, lingering here,
Shall add, to life's abounding joy,
  The charmed repose to suffering dear.

Still waits kind Nature to impart
  Her choicest gifts to such as gain
An entrance to her loving heart
  Through the sharp discipline of pain.

Forever from the Hand that takes
  One blessing from us others fall;

And, soon or late, our Father makes
　　His perfect recompense to all!

Oh, watched by Silence and the Night,
　　And folded in the strong embrace
Of the great mountains, with the light
　　Of the sweet heavens upon thy face,

Lake of the Northland! keep thy dower
　　Of beauty still, and while above
Thy solemn mountains speak of power,
　　Be thou the mirror of God's love.

SUNSET ON THE BEARCAMP

A GOLD fringe on the purpling hem
　　Of hills the river runs,
As down its long, green valley falls
　　The last of summer's suns.
Along its tawny gravel-bed
　　Broad-flowing, swift, and still,
As if its meadow levels felt
　　The hurry of the hill,
Noiseless between its banks of green
　　From curve to curve it slips;
The drowsy maple-shadows rest
　　Like fingers on its lips.

A waif from Carroll's wildest hills,
　　Unstoried and unknown;
The ursine legend of its name
　　Prowls on its banks alone.

Yet flowers as fair its slopes adorn
  As ever Yarrow knew,
Or, under rainy Irish skies,
  By Spenser's Mulla grew;
And through the gaps of leaning trees
  Its mountain cradle shows:
The gold against the amethyst,
  The green against the rose.

Touched by a light that hath no name,
  A glory never sung,
Aloft on sky and mountain wall
  Are God's great pictures hung.
How changed the summits vast and old!
  No longer granite-browed,
They melt in rosy mist; the rock
  Is softer than the cloud;
The valley holds its breath; no leaf
  Of all its elms is twirled:
The silence of eternity
  Seems falling on the world.

The pause before the breaking seals
  Of mystery is this;
Yon miracle-play of night and day
  Makes dumb its witnesses.
What unseen altar crowns the hills
  That reach up stair on stair?
What eyes look through, what white wings fan
  These purple veils of air?
What Presence from the heavenly heights
  To those of earth stoops down?

Not vainly Hellas dreamed of gods
  On Ida's snowy crown!

Slow fades the vision of the sky,
  The golden water pales,
And over all the valley-land
  A gray-winged vapor sails.
I go the common way of all;
  The sunset fires will burn,
The flowers will blow, the river flow,
  When I no more return.
No whisper from the mountain pine
  Nor lapsing stream shall tell
The stranger, treading where I tread,
  Of him who loved them well.

But beauty seen is never lost,
  God's colors all are fast;
The glory of this sunset heaven
  Into my soul has passed,
A sense of gladness unconfined
  To mortal date or clime;
As the soul liveth, it shall live
  Beyond the years of time.
Beside the mystic asphodels
  Shall bloom the home-born flowers,
And new horizons flush and glow
  With sunset hues of ours.

Farewell! these smiling hills must wear
  Too soon their wintry frown,
And snow-cold winds from off them shake
  The maple's red leaves down.

But I shall see a summer sun
  Still setting broad and low;
The mountain slopes shall blush and bloom,
  The golden water flow.
A lover's claim is mine on all
  I see to have and hold, —
The rose-light of perpetual hills,
  And sunsets never cold!

THE LAST WALK IN AUTUMN

I

O'ER the bare woods, whose outstretched hands
  Plead with the leaden heavens in vain,
I see, beyond the valley lands,
  The sea's long level dim with rain.
Around me all things, stark and dumb,
Seem praying for the snows to come,
And, for the summer bloom and greenness gone,
With winter's sunset lights and dazzling morn
    atone.

II

Along the river's summer walk,
  The withered tufts of asters nod;
And trembles on its arid stalk
  The hoar plume of the golden-rod.
And on a ground of sombre fir,
And azure-studded juniper,
The silver birch its buds of purple shows,
And scarlet berries tell where bloomed the sweet
    wild-rose!

III

With mingled sound of horns and bells,
  A far-heard clang, the wild geese fly,
Storm-sent, from Arctic moors and fells,
  Like a great arrow through the sky,
Two dusky lines converged in one,
Chasing the southward-flying sun;
While the brave snow-bird and the hardy jay
Call to them from the pines, as if to bid them stay.

IV

I passed this way a year ago:
  The wind blew south; the noon of day
Was warm as June's; and save that snow
  Flecked the low mountains far away,
And that the vernal-seeming breeze
Mocked faded grass and leafless trees,
I might have dreamed of summer as I lay,
Watching the fallen leaves with the soft wind at play.

V

Since then, the winter blasts have piled
  The white pagodas of the snow
On these rough slopes, and, strong and wild,
  Yon river, in its overflow
Of spring-time rain and sun, set free,
Crashed with its ices to the sea;
And over these gray fields, then green and gold,
The summer corn has waved, the thunder's organ rolled.

VI

Rich gift of God! A year of time!
    What pomp of rise and shut of day,
What hues wherewith our Northern clime
    Makes autumn's dropping woodlands gay,
What airs outblown from ferny dells,
And clover-bloom and sweetbrier smells,
What songs of brooks and birds, what fruits and
    flowers,
Green woods and moonlit snows, have in its round
    been ours!

VII

I know not how, in other lands,
    The changing seasons come and go;
What splendors fall on Syrian sands,
    What purple lights on Alpine snow!
Nor how the pomp of sunrise waits
On Venice at her watery gates;
A dream alone to me is Arno's vale,
And the Alhambra's halls are but a traveller's
    tale.

VIII

Yet, on life's current, he who drifts
    Is one with him who rows or sails;
And he who wanders widest lifts
    No more of beauty's jealous veils
Than he who from his doorway sees
The miracle of flowers and trees,
Feels the warm Orient in the noonday air,
And from cloud minarets hears the sunset call to
    prayer!

IX

The eye may well be glad that looks
    Where Pharpar's fountains rise and fall;
But he who sees his native brooks
    Laugh in the sun, has seen them all.
The marble palaces of Ind
    Rise round him in the snow and wind;
From his lone sweetbrier Persian Hafiz smiles,
And Rome's cathedral awe is in his woodland
    aisles.

X

And thus it is my fancy blends
    The near at hand and far and rare;
And while the same horizon bends
    Above the silver-sprinkled hair
Which flashed the light of morning skies
    On childhood's wonder-lifted eyes,
Within its round of sea and sky and field,
Earth wheels with all her zones, the Kosmos stands
    revealed.

XI

And thus the sick man on his bed,
    The toiler to his task-work bound,
Behold their prison-walls outspread,
    Their clipped horizon widen round!
While freedom-giving fancy waits,
    Like Peter's angel at the gates,
The power is theirs to baffle care and pain,
To bring the lost world back, and make it theirs
    again!

XII

What lack of goodly company,
    When masters of the ancient lyre
Obey my call, and trace for me
    Their words of mingled tears and fire!
I talk with Bacon, grave and wise,
I read the world with Pascal's eyes;
And priest and sage, with solemn brows austere,
And poets, garland-bound, the Lords of Thought, draw near.

XIII

Methinks, O friend, I hear thee say,
    "In vain the human heart we mock;
Bring living guests who love the day,
    Not ghosts who fly at crow of cock!
The herbs we share with flesh and blood
Are better than ambrosial food
With laurelled shades." I grant it, nothing loath,
But doubly blest is he who can partake of both.

XIV

He who might Plato's banquet grace,
    Have I not seen before me sit,
And watched his puritanic face,
    With more than Eastern wisdom lit?
Shrewd mystic! who, upon the back
Of his Poor Richard's Almanac
Writing the Sufi's song, the Gentoo's dream,
Links Manu's age of thought to Fulton's age of steam!

XV

Here too, of answering love secure,
  Have I not welcomed to my hearth
The gentle pilgrim troubadour,
  Whose songs have girdled half the earth;
Whose pages, like the magic mat
Whereon the Eastern lover sat,
Have borne me over Rhine-land's purple vines,
And Nubia's tawny sands, and Phrygia's mountain
    pines!

XVI

And he, who to the lettered wealth
  Of ages adds the lore unpriced,
The wisdom and the moral health,
  The ethics of the school of Christ;
The statesman to his holy trust,
As the Athenian archon, just,
Struck down, exiled like him for truth alone,
Has he not graced my home with beauty all his
    own?

XVII

What greetings smile, what farewells wave,
  What loved ones enter and depart!
The good, the beautiful, the brave,
  The Heaven-lent treasures of the heart!
How conscious seems the frozen sod
And beechen slope whereon they trod!
The oak-leaves rustle, and the dry grass bends
Beneath the shadowy feet of lost or absent
    friends.

XXIV

Here manhood struggles for the sake
  Of mother, sister, daughter, wife,
The graces and the loves which make
  The music of the march of life;
And woman, in her daily round
Of duty, walks on holy ground.
No unpaid menial tills the soil, nor here
Is the bad lesson learned at human rights to
    sneer.

XXV

Then let the icy north-wind blow
  The trumpets of the coming storm,
To arrowy sleet and blinding snow
  Yon slanting lines of rain transform.
Young hearts shall hail the drifted cold,
As gayly as I did of old;
And I, who watch them through the frosty pane,
Unenvious, live in them my boyhood o'er again.

XXVI

And I will trust that He who heeds
  The life that hides in mead and wold,
Who hangs yon alder's crimson beads,
  And stains these mosses green and gold,
Will still, as He hath done, incline
His gracious care to me and mine;
Grant what we ask aright, from wrong debar,
And, as the earth grows dark, make brighter
    every star!

XVIII

Then ask not why to these bleak hills
  I cling, as clings the tufted moss,
To bear the winter's lingering chills,
  The mocking spring's perpetual loss.
I dream of lands where summer smiles,
And soft winds blow from spicy isles,
But scarce would Ceylon's breath of flowers be
    sweet,
Could I not feel thy soil, New England, at my feet!

XIX

At times I long for gentler skies,
  And bathe in dreams of softer air,
But homesick tears would fill the eyes
  That saw the Cross without the Bear.
The pine must whisper to the palm,
The north-wind break the tropic calm;
And with the dreamy languor of the Line,
The North's keen virtue blend, and strength to
    beauty join.

XX

Better to stem with heart and hand
  The roaring tide of life, than lie,
Unmindful, on its flowery strand,
  Of God's occasions drifting by!
Better with naked nerve to bear
The needles of this goading air,
Than, in the lap of sensual ease, forego
The godlike power to do, the godlike aim to know.

XXI

Home of my heart! to me more fai[r]
  Than gay Versailles or Windsor'[s]
The painted, shingly town-house w[here]
  The freeman's vote for Freedom
The simple roof where prayer is ma[de]
Than Gothic groin and colonnade;
The living temple of the heart of ma[n]
Than Rome's sky-mocking vault, or
    Milan!

XXII

More dear thy equal village schools
  Where rich and poor the Bible re[ad]
Than classic halls where Priestcraf[t]
  And Learning wears the chains
Thy glad Thanksgiving, gathering
The scattered sheaves of home and
Than the mad license ushering Lent
Or holidays of slaves who laugh
    chains.

XXIII

And sweet homes nestle in these d
  And perch along these wooded s
And, blest beyond Arcadian vales,
  They hear the sound of Sabbath
Here dwells no perfect man sublim[e]
Nor woman winged before her tim[e]
But with the faults and follies of th
Old home-bred virtues hold their
    place.

XXVII

I have not seen, I may not see,
  My hopes for man take form in fact,
But God will give the victory
  In due time; in that faith I act.
And he who sees the future sure,
The baffling present may endure,
And bless, meanwhile, the unseen Hand that leads
The heart's desires beyond the halting step of
    deeds.

XXVIII

And thou, my song, I send thee forth,
  Where harsher songs of mine have flown;
Go, find a place at home and hearth
  Where'er thy singer's name is known;
Revive for him the kindly thought
Of friends; and they who love him not,
Touched by some strain of thine, perchance may
    take
The hand he proffers all, and thank him for thy
    sake.

AN OUTDOOR RECEPTION

The substance of these lines, hastily pencilled several years ago, I find among such of my unprinted scraps as have escaped the waste-basket and the fire. In transcribing it I have made some changes, additions, and omissions.

O<small>N</small> these green banks, where falls too soon
  The shade of Autumn's afternoon,

AN OUTDOOR RECEPTION

The south wind blowing soft and sweet,
The water gliding at my feet,
The distant northern range uplit
By the slant sunshine over it,
With changes of the mountain mist
From tender blush to amethyst,
The valley's stretch of shade and gleam
Fair as in Mirza's Bagdad dream,
With glad young faces smiling near
And merry voices in my ear,
I sit, methinks, as Hafiz might
In Iran's Garden of Delight.
For Persian roses blushing red,
Aster and gentian bloom instead;
For Shiraz wine, this mountain air;
For feast, the blueberries which I share
With one who proffers with stained hands
Her gleanings from yon pasture lands,
Wild fruit that art and culture spoil,
The harvest of an untilled soil;
And with her one whose tender eyes
Reflect the change of April skies,
Midway 'twixt child and maiden yet,
Fresh as Spring's earliest violet;
And one whose look and voice and ways
Make where she goes idyllic days;
And one whose sweet, still countenance
Seems dreamful of a child's romance;
And others, welcome as are these,
Like and unlike, varieties
Of pearls on nature's chaplet strung,
And all are fair, for all are young.

AN OUTDOOR RECEPTION

Gathered from seaside cities old,
From midland prairie, lake, and wold,
From the great wheat-fields, which might feed
The hunger of a world at need,
In healthful change of rest and play
Their school-vacations glide away.

No critics these: they only see
An old and kindly friend in me,
In whose amused, indulgent look
Their innocent mirth has no rebuke.
They scarce can know my rugged rhymes,
The harsher songs of evil times,
Nor graver themes in minor keys
Of life's and death's solemnities;
But haply, as they bear in mind
Some verse of lighter, happier kind, —
Hints of the boyhood of the man,
Youth viewed from life's meridian,
Half seriously and half in play
My pleasant interviewers pay
Their visit, with no fell intent
Of taking notes and punishment.

As yonder solitary pine
Is ringed below with flower and vine,
More favored than that lonely tree,
The bloom of girlhood circles me.
In such an atmosphere of youth
I half forget my age's truth;
The shadow of my life's long date
Runs backward on the dial-plate,

Until it seems a step might span
The gulf between the boy and man.

My young friends smile, as if some jay
On bleak December's leafless spray
Essayed to sing the songs of May.
Well, let them smile, and live to know,
When their brown locks are flecked with snow
'T is tedious to be always sage
And pose the dignity of age,
While so much of our early lives
On memory's playground still survives,
And owns, as at the present hour,
The spell of youth's magnetic power.

But though I feel, with Solomon,
'T is pleasant to behold the sun,
I would not if I could repeat
A life which still is good and sweet;
I keep in age, as in my prime,
A not uncheerful step with time,
And, grateful for all blessings sent,
I go the common way, content
To make no new experiment.
On easy terms with law and fate,
For what must be I calmly wait,
And trust the path I cannot see, —
That God is good sufficeth me.
And when at last on life's strange play
The curtain falls, I only pray
That hope may lose itself in truth,
And age in Heaven's immortal youth,

And all our loves and longing prove
The foretaste of diviner love!

The day is done. Its afterglow
Along the west is burning low.
My visitors, like birds, have flown;
I hear their voices, fainter grown,
And dimly through the dusk I see
Their kerchiefs wave good-night to me, —
Light hearts of girlhood, knowing naught
Of all the cheer their coming brought;
And, in their going, unaware
Of silent-falling feet of prayer:
Heaven make their budding promise good
With flowers of gracious womanhood!

THE TENT ON THE BEACH

It can scarcely be necessary to name as the two companions whom I reckoned with myself in this poetical picnic, Fields the lettered magnate, and Taylor the free cosmopolite. The long line of sandy beach which defines almost the whole of the New Hampshire sea-coast is especially marked, near its southern extremity, by the salt-meadows of Hampton. The Hampton River winds through these meadows, and the reader may, if he choose, imagine my tent pitched near its mouth, where also was the scene of the *Wreck of Rivermouth*. The green bluff to the northward is Great Boar's Head; southward is the Merrimac, with Newburyport lifting its steeples above brown roofs and green trees on its banks. [Mr. Whittier originally designed following the Decameron method and feigning that each person read his own poem, but abandoned it as too hackneyed.]

I WOULD not sin, in this half-playful strain, —
  Too light perhaps for serious years, though born
Of the enforcèd leisure of slow pain, —
  Against the pure ideal which has drawn
My feet to follow its far-shining gleam.
A simple plot is mine: legends and runes
Of credulous days, old fancies that have lain
Silent from boyhood taking voice again,
Warmed into life once more, even as the tunes
That, frozen in the fabled hunting-horn,
Thawed into sound: — a winter fireside dream
Of dawns and sunsets by the summer sea,
Whose sands are traversed by a silent throng
Of voyagers from that vaster mystery
Of which it is an emblem; — and the dear
Memory of one who might have tuned my song
To sweeter music by her delicate ear.

When heats as of a tropic clime
  Burned all our inland valleys through,
Three friends, the guests of summer time,
  Pitched their white tent where sea-winds blew.
Behind them, marshes, seamed and crossed
  With narrow creeks, and flower-embossed,
Stretched to the dark oak wood, whose leafy arms
Screened from the stormy East the pleasant inland farms.

At full of tide their bolder shore
  Of sun-bleached sand the waters beat;
At ebb, a smooth and glistening floor
  They touched with light, receding feet.
Northward a green bluff broke the chain
Of sand-hills; southward stretched a plain
Of salt grass, with a river winding down,
Sail - whitened, and beyond the steeples of the
    town, —

Whence sometimes, when the wind was light
  And dull the thunder of the beach,
They heard the bells of morn and night
  Swing, miles away, their silver speech.
Above low scarp and turf-grown wall
They saw the fort-flag rise and fall;
And, the first star to signal twilight's hour,
The lamp-fire glimmer down from the tall light-
    house tower.

They rested there, escaped awhile
  From cares that wear the life away,
To eat the lotus of the Nile
  And drink the poppies of Cathay, —
To fling their loads of custom down,
Like drift-weed, on the sand-slopes brown,
And in the sea-waves drown the restless pack
Of duties, claims, and needs that barked upon
    their track.

One, with his beard scarce silvered, bore
  A ready credence in his looks,

A lettered magnate, lording o'er
   An ever-widening realm of books.
In him brain-currents, near and far,
   Converged as in a Leyden jar;
The old, dead authors thronged him round about,
And Elzevir's gray ghosts from leathern graves
   looked out.

He knew each living pundit well,
   Could weigh the gifts of him or her,
And well the market value tell
   Of poet and philosopher.
But if he lost, the scenes behind,
Somewhat of reverence vague and blind,
Finding the actors human at the best,
No readier lips than his the good he saw confessed.

His boyhood fancies not outgrown,
   He loved himself the singer's art;
Tenderly, gently, by his own
   He knew and judged an author's heart.
No Rhadamanthine brow of doom
Bowed the dazed pedant from his room;
And bards, whose name is legion, if denied,
Bore off alike intact their verses and their pride.

Pleasant it was to roam about
   The lettered world as he had done,
And see the lords of song without
   Their singing robes and garlands on.
With Wordsworth paddle Rydal mere,
Taste rugged Elliott's home-brewed beer,

And with the ears of Rogers, at fourscore,
Hear Garrick's buskined tread and Walpole's wit
    once more.

And one there was, a dreamer born,
    Who, with a mission to fulfil,
Had left the Muses' haunts to turn
    The crank of an opinion-mill,
Making his rustic reed of song
A weapon in the war with wrong,
Yoking his fancy to the breaking-plough
That beam-deep turned the soil for truth to spring
    and grow.

Too quiet seemed the man to ride
    The wingèd Hippogriff Reform;
Was his a voice from side to side
    To pierce the tumult of the storm?
A silent, shy, peace-loving man,
He seemed no fiery partisan
To hold his way against the public frown,
The ban of Church and State, the fierce mob's
    hounding down.

For while he wrought with strenuous will
    The work his hands had found to do,
He heard the fitful music still
    Of winds that out of dream-land blew.
The din about him could not drown
What the strange voices whispered down;
Along his task-field weird processions swept,
The visionary pomp of stately phantoms stepped.

The common air was thick with dreams, —
  He told them to the toiling crowd;
Such music as the woods and streams
  Sang in his ear he sang aloud;
In still, shut bays, on windy capes,
He heard the call of beckoning shapes,
And, as the gray old shadows prompted him,
To homely moulds of rhyme he shaped their legends grim.

He rested now his weary hands,
  And lightly moralized and laughed,
As, tracing on the shifting sands
  A burlesque of his paper-craft,
He saw the careless waves o'errun
His words, as time before had done,
Each day's tide-water washing clean away,
Like letters from the sand, the work of yesterday.

And one, whose Arab face was tanned
  By tropic sun and boreal frost,
So travelled there was scarce a land
  Or people left him to exhaust,
In idling mood had from him hurled
The poor squeezed orange of the world,
And in the tent-shade, sat beneath a palm,
Smoked, cross-legged like a Turk, in Oriental calm.

The very waves that washed the sand
  Below him, he had seen before
Whitening the Scandinavian strand
  And sultry Mauritanian shore.

From ice-rimmed isles, from summer seas
  Palm-fringed, they bore him messages ;
He heard the plaintive Nubian songs again,
And mule-bells tinkling down the mountain-paths
    of Spain.

His memory round the ransacked earth
  On Puck's long girdle slid at ease;
And, instant, to the valley's girth
  Of mountains, spice isles of the seas,
Faith flowered in minster stones, Art's guess
  At truth and beauty, found access ;
Yet loved the while, that free cosmopolite,
Old friends, old ways, and kept his boyhood's
    dreams in sight.

Untouched as yet by wealth and pride,
  That virgin innocence of beach :
No shingly monster, hundred-eyed,
  Stared its gray sand-birds out of reach ;
Unhoused, save where, at intervals,
  The white tents showed their canvas walls,
Where brief sojourners, in the cool, soft air,
Forgot their inland heats, hard toil, and year-long
    care.

Sometimes along the wheel-deep sand
  A one-horse wagon slowly crawled,
Deep laden with a youthful band,
  Whose look some homestead old recalled;
Brother perchance, and sisters twain,
And one whose blue eyes told, more plain

Than the free language of her rosy lip,
Of the still dearer claim of love's relationship.

With cheeks of russet-orchard tint,
　　The light laugh of their native rills,
The perfume of their garden's mint,
　　The breezy freedom of the hills,
They bore, in unrestrained delight,
　　The motto of the Garter's knight,
Careless as if from every gazing thing
Hid by their innocence, as Gyges by his ring.

The clanging sea-fowl came and went,
　　The hunter's gun in the marshes rang;
At nightfall from a neighboring tent
　　A flute-voiced woman sweetly sang.
Loose-haired, barefooted, hand-in-hand,
　　Young girls went tripping down the sand;
And youths and maidens, sitting in the moon,
Dreamed o'er the old fond dream from which we
　　wake too soon.

At times their fishing-lines they plied,
　　With an old Triton at the oar,
Salt as the sea-wind, tough and dried
　　As a lean cusk from Labrador.
Strange tales he told of wreck and storm, —
　　Had seen the sea-snake's awful form,
And heard the ghosts on Haley's Isle complain,
Speak him off shore, and beg a passage to old
　　Spain!

And there, on breezy morns, they saw
  The fishing-schooners outward run,
Their low-bent sails in tack and flaw
  Turned white or dark to shade and sun.
Sometimes, in calms of closing day,
They watched the spectral mirage play,
Saw low, far islands looming tall and nigh,
And ships, with upturned keels, sail like a sea the
    sky.

Sometimes a cloud, with thunder black,
  Stooped low upon the darkening main,
Piercing the waves along its track
  With the slant javelins of rain.
And when west-wind and sunshine warm
Chased out to sea its wrecks of storm,
They saw the prismy hues in thin spray showers
Where the green buds of waves burst into white
    froth flowers.

And when along the line of shore
  The mists crept upward chill and damp,
Stretched, careless, on their sandy floor
  Beneath the flaring lantern lamp,
They talked of all things old and new,
Read, slept, and dreamed as idlers do;
And in the unquestioned freedom of the tent,
Body and o'er-taxed mind to healthful ease un-
    bent.

Once, when the sunset splendors died,
  And, trampling up the sloping sand,

In lines outreaching far and wide,
  The white-maned billows swept to land,
Dim seen across the gathering shade,
A vast and ghostly cavalcade,
They sat around their lighted kerosene,
Hearing the deep bass roar their every pause between.

Then, urged thereto, the Editor
  Within his full portfolio dipped,
Feigning excuse while searching for
  (With secret pride) his manuscript.
His pale face flushed from eye to beard,
With nervous cough his throat he cleared.
And, in a voice so tremulous it betrayed
The anxious fondness of an author's heart, he
  read:

THE WRECK OF RIVERMOUTH

The Goody Cole who figures in this poem and *The Changeling* was Eunice Cole, who for a quarter of a century or more was feared, persecuted, and hated as the witch of Hampton. She lived alone in a hovel a little distant from the spot where the Hampton Academy now stands, and there she died, unattended. When her death was discovered, she was hastily covered up in the earth near by, and a stake driven through her body, to exorcise the evil spirit. [When Goody Cole was brought before the Quarter Sessions in 1680 to answer to the charge of being a witch, the court could not find satisfactory evidence of witchcraft, but so strong was the feeling against her that Major Waldron, the presiding magistrate, ordered her to be imprisoned with a lock kept on her leg at the pleasure of the court. In such judicial action one can read the fear and vindictive spirit of the community at large.] Rev. Stephen Bachiler or Batchelder was one of the ablest of the early New England preachers. His marriage late in life to a woman regarded by his church as disreputable induced him to return to England, where he enjoyed the esteem and favor of Oliver Cromwell during the Protectorate.

RIVERMOUTH Rocks are fair to see,
  By dawn or sunset shone across,
When the ebb of the sea has left them free
  To dry their fringes of gold-green moss:
For there the river comes winding down,
From salt sea-meadows and uplands brown,
And waves on the outer rocks afoam
Shout to its waters, "Welcome home!"

And fair are the sunny isles in view
  East of the grisly Head of the Boar,
And Agamenticus lifts its blue
  Disk of a cloud the woodlands o'er;
And southerly, when the tide is down,
'Twixt white sea-waves and sand-hills brown,
The beach-birds dance and the gray gulls wheel
Over a floor of burnished steel.

Once, in the old Colonial days,
  Two hundred years ago and more,
A boat sailed down through the winding ways
  Of Hampton River to that low shore,
Full of a goodly company
Sailing out on the summer sea,
Veering to catch the land-breeze light,
With the Boar to left and the Rocks to right.

In Hampton meadows, where mowers laid
 Their scythes to the swaths of salted grass,
"Ah, well-a-day! our hay must be made!"
 A young man sighed, who saw them pass.
Loud laughed his fellows to see him stand
Whetting his scythe with a listless hand,
Hearing a voice in a far-off song,
Watching a white hand beckoning long.

"Fie on the witch!" cried a merry girl,
 As they rounded the point where Goody Cole
Sat by her door with her wheel atwirl,
 A bent and blear-eyed poor old soul.
"Oho!" she muttered, "ye 're brave to-day!
But I hear the little waves laugh and say,
'The broth will be cold that waits at home;
For it 's one to go, but another to come!'"

"She 's cursed," said the skipper; "speak her fair:
I 'm scary always to see her shake
Her wicked head, with its wild gray hair,
 And nose like a hawk, and eyes like a snake."
But merrily still, with laugh and shout,
From Hampton River the boat sailed out,
Till the huts and the flakes on Star seemed nigh,
And they lost the scent of the pines of Rye.

They dropped their lines in the lazy tide,
 Drawing up haddock and mottled cod;
They saw not the Shadow that walked beside,
 They heard not the feet with silence shod.

THE WRECK OF RIVERMOUTH

But thicker and thicker a hot mist grew,
Shot by the lightnings through and through;
And muffled growls, like the growl of a beast,
Ran along the sky from west to east.

Then the skipper looked from the darkening sea
　Up to the dimmed and wading sun;
But he spake like a brave man cheerily,
　"Yet there is time for our homeward run."
Veering and tacking, they backward wore;
And just as a breath from the woods ashore
Blew out to whisper of danger past,
The wrath of the storm came down at last!

The skipper hauled at the heavy sail:
　"God be our help!" he only cried,
As the roaring gale, like the stroke of a flail,
　Smote the boat on its starboard side.
The Shoalsmen looked, but saw alone
Dark films of rain-cloud slantwise blown,
Wild rocks lit up by the lightning's glare,
The strife and torment of sea and air.

Goody Cole looked out from her door:
　The Isles of Shoals were drowned and gone,
Scarcely she saw the Head of the Boar
　Toss the foam from tusks of stone.
She clasped her hands with a grip of pain,
The tear on her cheek was not of rain:
"They are lost," she muttered, "boat and crew!
Lord, forgive me! my words were true!"

Suddenly seaward swept the squall;
   The low sun smote through cloudy rack;
The Shoals stood clear in the light, and all
   The trend of the coast lay hard and black.
But far and wide as eye could reach,
No life was seen upon wave or beach;
The boat that went out at morning never
Sailed back again into Hampton River.

O mower, lean on thy bended snath,
   Look from the meadows green and low:
The wind of the sea is a waft of death,
   The waves are singing a song of woe!
By silent river, by moaning sea,
Long and vain shall thy watching be:
Never again shall the sweet voice call,
Never the white hand rise and fall!

O Rivermouth Rocks, how sad a sight
   Ye saw in the light of breaking day!
Dead faces looking up cold and white
   From sand and seaweed where they lay.
The mad old witch-wife wailed and wept,
And cursed the tide as it backward crept:
"Crawl back, crawl back, blue water-snake!
Leave your dead for the hearts that break!"

Solemn it was in that old day
   In Hampton town and its log-built church,
Where side by side the coffins lay
   And the mourners stood in aisle and porch

In the singing-seats young eyes were dim,
The voices faltered that raised the hymn,
And Father Dalton, grave and stern,
Sobbed through his prayer and wept in turn.

But his ancient colleague did not pray;
  Under the weight of his fourscore years
He stood apart with the iron-gray
  Of his strong brows knitted to hide his tears;
And a fair-faced woman of doubtful fame,
Linking her own with his honored name,
Subtle as sin, at his side withstood
The felt reproach of her neighborhood.

Apart with them, like them forbid,
  Old Goody Cole looked drearily round,
As, two by two, with their faces hid,
  The mourners walked to the burying-ground.
She let the staff from her clasped hands fall:
"Lord, forgive us! we 're sinners all!"
And the voice of the old man answered her:
"Amen!" said Father Bachiler.

So, as I sat upon Appledore
  In the calm of a closing summer day,
And the broken lines of Hampton shore
  In purple mist of cloudland lay,
The Rivermouth Rocks their story told;
And waves aglow with sunset gold,
Rising and breaking in steady chime,
Beat the rhythm and kept the time.

And the sunset paled, and warmed once more
  With a softer, tenderer after-glow;
In the east was moon-rise, with boats off-shore
  And sails in the distance drifting slow.
The beacon glimmered from Portsmouth bar,
The White Isle kindled its great red star;
And life and death in my old-time lay
Mingled in peace like the night and day!

"Well!" said the Man of Books, "your story
  Is really not ill told in verse.
As the Celt said of purgatory,
  One might go farther and fare worse."
The Reader smiled; and once again
With steadier voice took up his strain,
While the fair singer from the neighboring tent
Drew near, and at his side a graceful listener bent.

THE GRAVE BY THE LAKE

At the mouth of the Melvin River, which empties into Moultonboro Bay in Lake Winnipesaukee, is a great mound. The Ossipee Indians had their home in the neighborhood of the bay, which is plentifully stocked with fish, and many relics of their occupation have been found.

WHERE the Great Lake's sunny smiles
  Dimple round its hundred isles,
And the mountain's granite ledge
  Cleaves the water like a wedge,
Ringed about with smooth, gray stones,
Rest the giant's mighty bones.

Close beside, in shade and gleam,
Laughs and ripples Melvin stream;
Melvin water, mountain-born,
All fair flowers its banks adorn;
All the woodland voices meet,
Mingling with its murmurs sweet.

Over lowlands forest-grown,
Over waters island-strown,
Over silver-sanded beach,
Leaf-locked bay and misty reach,
Melvin stream and burial-heap,
Watch and ward the mountains keep.

Who that Titan cromlech fills?
Forest-kaiser, lord o' the hills?
Knight who on the birchen tree
Carved his savage heraldry?
Priest o' the pine-wood temples dim,
Prophet, sage, or wizard grim?

Rugged type of primal man,
Grim utilitarian,
Loving woods for hunt and prowl,
Lake and hill for fish and fowl,
As the brown bear blind and dull
To the grand and beautiful:

Not for him the lesson drawn
From the mountains smit with dawn.
Star-rise, moon-rise, flowers of May,
Sunset's purple bloom of day, —

Took his life no hue from thence,
Poor amid such affluence?

Haply unto hill and tree
All too near akin was he:
Unto him who stands afar
Nature's marvels greatest are;
Who the mountain purple seeks
Must not climb the higher peaks.

Yet who knows, in winter tramp,
Or the midnight of the camp,
What revealings faint and far,
Stealing down from moon and star,
Kindled in that human clod
Thought of destiny and God?

Stateliest forest patriarch,
Grand in robes of skin and bark,
What sepulchral mysteries,
What weird funeral-rites, were his?
What sharp wail, what drear lament,
Back scared wolf and eagle sent?

Now, whate'er he may have been,
Low he lies as other men;
On his mound the partridge drums,
There the noisy blue-jay comes;
Rank nor name nor pomp has he
In the grave's democracy.

Part thy blue lips, Northern lake!
Moss-grown rocks, your silence break!

Tell the tale, thou ancient tree!
Thou, too, slide-worn Ossipee!
Speak, and tell us how and when
Lived and died this king of men!

Wordless moans the ancient pine;
Lake and mountain give no sign;
Vain to trace this ring of stones;
Vain the search of crumbling bones:
Deepest of all mysteries,
And the saddest, silence is.

Nameless, noteless, clay with clay
Mingles slowly day by day;
But somewhere, for good or ill,
That dark soul is living still;
Somewhere yet that atom's force
Moves the light-poised universe.

Strange that on his burial-sod
Harebells bloom, and golden-rod,
While the soul's dark horoscope
Holds no starry sign of hope!
Is the Unseen with sight at odds?
Nature's pity more than God's?

Thus I mused by Melvin's side,
While the summer eventide
Made the woods and inland sea
And the mountains mystery;
And the hush of earth and air
Seemed the pause before a prayer, —

Prayer for him, for all who rest,
Mother Earth, upon thy breast, —
Lapped on Christian turf, or hid
In rock-cave or pyramid:
All who sleep, as all who live,
Well may need the prayer, "Forgive!"

Desert-smothered caravan,
Knee-deep dust that once was man,
Battle-trenches ghastly piled,
Ocean-floors with white bones tiled,
Crowded tomb and mounded sod,
Dumbly crave that prayer to God.

Oh, the generations old
Over whom no church-bells tolled,
Christless, lifting up blind eyes
To the silence of the skies!
For the innumerable dead
Is my soul disquieted.

Where be now these silent hosts?
Where the camping-ground of ghosts?
Where the spectral conscripts led
To the white tents of the dead?
What strange shore or chartless sea
Holds the awful mystery?

Then the warm sky stooped to make
Double sunset in the lake;
While above I saw with it,
Range on range, the mountains lit;

THE GRAVE BY THE LAKE

And the calm and splendor stole
Like an answer to my soul.

Hear'st thou, O of little faith,
What to thee the mountain saith,
What is whispered by the trees? —
Cast on God thy care for these;
Trust Him, if thy sight be dim:
Doubt for them is doubt of Him.

Blind must be their close-shut eyes
Where like night the sunshine lies,
Fiery-linked the self-forged chain
Binding ever sin to pain,
Strong their prison-house of will,
But without He waiteth still.

Not with hatred's undertow
Doth the Love Eternal flow;
Every chain that spirits wear
Crumbles in the breath of prayer;
And the penitent's desire
Opens every gate of fire.

Still Thy love, O Christ arisen,
Yearns to reach these souls in prison!
Through all depths of sin and loss
Drops the plummet of Thy cross!
Never yet abyss was found
Deeper than that cross could sound!"

Therefore well may Nature keep
Equal faith with all who sleep,

Set her watch of hills around
Christian grave and heathen mound,
And to cairn and kirkyard send
Summer's flowery dividend.

Keep, O pleasant Melvin stream,
Thy sweet laugh in shade and gleam!
On the Indian's grassy tomb
Swing, O flowers, your bells of bloom!
Deep below, as high above,
Sweeps the circle of God's love.

He paused and questioned with his eye
  The hearers' verdict on his song.
A low voice asked: "Is 't well to pry
  Into the secrets which belong
Only to God? — The life to be
Is still the unguessed mystery:
Unscaled, unpierced the cloudy walls remain,
We beat with dream and wish the soundless doors
  in vain.

"But faith beyond our sight may go."
  He said: "The gracious Fatherhood
Can only know above, below,
  Eternal purposes of good.
From our free heritage of will,
  The bitter springs of pain and ill
Flow only in all worlds. The perfect day
Of God is shadowless, and love is love alway."

"I know," she said, "the letter kills;
  That on our arid fields of strife
And heat of clashing texts distils
  The dew of spirit and of life.
But, searching still the written Word,
I fain would find, Thus saith the Lord,
A voucher for the hope I also feel
That sin can give no wound beyond love's power
    to heal."

"Pray," said the Man of Books, "give o'er
  A theme too vast for time and place.
Go on, Sir Poet, ride once more
  Your hobby at his old free pace.
But let him keep, with step discreet,
The solid earth beneath his feet.
In the great mystery which around us lies,
The wisest is a fool, the fool Heaven-helped is
    wise."

The Traveller said: "If songs have creeds,
  Their choice of them let singers make;
But Art no other sanction needs
  Than beauty for its own fair sake.
It grinds not in the mill of use,
Nor asks for leave, nor begs excuse;
It makes the flexile laws it deigns to own,
And gives its atmosphere its color and its tone.

"Confess, old friend, your austere school
  Has left your fancy little chance;
You square to reason's rigid rule
  The flowing outlines of romance.

With conscience keen from exercise,
  And chronic fear of compromise,
You check the free play of your rhymes, to clap
A moral underneath, and spring it like a trap."

The sweet voice answered : " Better so
  Than bolder flights that know no check;
Better to use the bit, than throw
  The reins all loose on fancy's neck.
The liberal range of Art should be
  The breadth of Christian liberty,
Restrained alone by challenge and alarm
Where its charmed footsteps tread the border land
    of harm.

" Beyond the poet's sweet dream lives
  The eternal epic of the man.
He wisest is who only gives,
  True to himself, the best he can;
Who, drifting in the winds of praise,
  The inward monitor obeys;
And, with the boldness that confesses fear,
Takes in the crowded sail, and lets his conscience
    steer.

" Thanks for the fitting word he speaks,
  Nor less for doubtful word unspoken,
For the false model that he breaks,
  As for the moulded grace unbroken;
For what is missed and what remains,
For losses which are truest gains,
For reverence conscious of the Eternal eye,
And truth too fair to need the garnish of a lie."

Laughing, the Critic bowed. "I yield
   The point without another word;
Who ever yet a case appealed
   Where beauty's judgment had been heard?
And you, my good friend, owe to me
Your warmest thanks for such a plea,
As true withal as sweet. For my offence
Of cavil, let her words be ample recompense."

Across the sea one lighthouse star,
   With crimson ray that came and went,
Revolving on its tower afar,
   Looked through the doorway of the tent.
While outward, over sand-slopes wet,
The lamp flashed down its yellow jet
On the long wash of waves, with red and green
Tangles of weltering weed through the white foam-
      wreaths seen.

"'Sing while we may, — another day
   May bring enough of sorrow;'— thus
Our Traveller in his own sweet lay,
   His Crimean camp-song, hints to us,"
The lady said. "So let it be;
Sing us a song," exclaimed all three.
She smiled: "I can but marvel at your choice
To hear our poet's words through my poor bor-
      rowed voice."

         Her window opens to the bay,
         On glistening light or misty gray,
         And there at dawn and set of day
            In prayer she kneels.

"Dear Lord!" she saith, "to many a home
From wind and wave the wanderers come
I only see the tossing foam
    Of stranger keels.

"Blown out and in by summer gales,
The stately ships, with crowded sails,
And sailors leaning o'er their rails,
    Before me glide;
They come, they go, but nevermore,
Spice-laden from the Indian shore,
I see his swift-winged Isidore
    The waves divide.

"O Thou! with whom the night is day
And one the near and far away,
Look out on yon gray waste, and say
    Where lingers he.
Alive, perchance, on some lone beach
Or thirsty isle beyond the reach
Of man, he hears the mocking speech
    Of wind and sea.

"O dread and cruel deep, reveal
The secret which thy waves conceal,
And, ye wild sea-birds, hither wheel
    And tell your tale.
Let winds that tossed his raven hair
A message from my lost one bear, —
Some thought of me, a last fond prayer
    Or dying wail!

"Come, with your dreariest truth shut out
 The fears that haunt me round about;
 O God! I cannot bear this doubt
  That stifles breath.
 The worst is better than the dread;
 Give me but leave to mourn my dead
 Asleep in trust and hope, instead
  Of life in death!"

It might have been the evening breeze
 That whispered in the garden trees,
 It might have been the sound of seas
  That rose and fell;
 But, with her heart, if not her ear,
 The old loved voice she seemed to hear:
 "I wait to meet thee: be of cheer,
  For all is well!"

———

The sweet voice into silence went,
 A silence which was almost pain
As through it rolled the long lament,
 The cadence of the mournful main.
Glancing his written pages o'er,
 The Reader tried his part once more;
Leaving the land of hackmatack and pine
For Tuscan valleys glad with olive and with vine.

THE BROTHER OF MERCY

PIERO LUCA, known of all the town
As the gray porter by the Pitti wall
Where the noon shadows of the gardens fall,
Sick and in dolor, waited to lay down
His last sad burden, and beside his mat
The barefoot monk of La Certosa sat.

Unseen, in square and blossoming garden drifted,
Soft sunset lights through green Val d' Arno sifted;
Unheard, below the living shuttles shifted
Backward and forth, and wove, in love or strife,
In mirth or pain, the mottled web of life:
But when at last came upward from the street
Tinkle of bell and tread of measured feet,
The sick man started, strove to rise in vain,
Sinking back heavily with a moan of pain.
And the monk said, " 'T is but the Brotherhood
Of Mercy going on some errand good:
Their black masks by the palace-wall I see."
Piero answered faintly, " Woe is me!
This day for the first time in forty years
In vain the bell hath sounded in my ears,
Calling me with my brethren of the mask,
Beggar and prince alike, to some new task
Of love or pity, — haply from the street
To bear a wretch plague-stricken, or, with feet
Hushed to the quickened ear and feverish brain,
To tread the crowded lazaretto's floors.

THE BROTHER OF MERCY

Down the long twilight of the corridors,
Midst tossing arms and faces full of pain.
I loved the work: it was its own reward.
I never counted on it to offset
My sins, which are many, or make less my debt
To the free grace and mercy of our Lord;
But somehow, father, it has come to be
In these long years so much a part of me,
I should not know myself, if lacking it,
But with the work the worker too would die,
And in my place some other self would sit
Joyful or sad, — what matters, if not I?
And now all's over. Woe is me!" — "My son,"
The monk said soothingly, "thy work is done;
And no more as a servant, but the guest
Of God, thou enterest thy eternal rest.
No toil, no tears, no sorrow for the lost,
Shall mar thy perfect bliss. Thou shalt sit down
Clad in white robes, and wear a golden crown
Forever and forever." — Piero tossed
On his sick-pillow: "Miserable me!
I am too poor for such grand company;
The crown would be too heavy for this gray
Old head; and God forgive me if I say
It would be hard to sit there night and day,
Like an image in the Tribune, doing naught
With these hard hands, that all my life have
    wrought,
Not for bread only, but for pity's sake.
I'm dull at prayers: I could not keep awake,
Counting my beads. Mine's but a crazy head,
Scarce worth the saving, if all else be dead.

And if one goes to heaven without a heart,
God knows he leaves behind his better part.
I love my fellow-men: the worst I know
I would do good to. Will death change me so
That I shall sit among the lazy saints,
Turning a deaf ear to the sore complaints
Of souls that suffer? Why, I never yet
Left a poor dog in the *strada* hard beset,
Or ass o'erladen! Must I rate man less
Than dog or ass, in holy selfishness?
Methinks (Lord, pardon, if the thought be sin!)
The world of pain were better, if therein
One's heart might still be human, and desires
Of natural pity drop upon its fires
Some cooling tears."
      Thereat the pale monk crossed
His brow, and muttering, "Madman! thou art
 lost!"
Took up his pyx and fled; and, left alone,
The sick man closed his eyes with a great groan
That sank into a prayer, "Thy will be done!"

Then was he made aware, by soul or ear,
Of somewhat pure and holy bending o'er him,
And of a voice like that of her who bore him,
Tender and most compassionate: "Never fear!
For heaven is love, as God himself is love;
Thy work below shall be thy work above."
And when he looked, lo! in the stern monk's
 place
He saw the shining of an angel's face!

The Traveller broke the pause. "I've seen
    The Brothers down the long street steal,
Black, silent, masked, the crowd between,
    And felt to doff my hat and kneel
With heart, if not with knee, in prayer,
For blessings on their pious care."
The Reader wiped his glasses: "Friends of mine,
We'll try our home-brewed next, instead of foreign wine."

THE CHANGELING

For the fairest maid in Hampton
    They needed not to search,
Who saw young Anna Favor
    Come walking into church,—

Or bringing from the meadows,
    At set of harvest-day,
The frolic of the blackbirds,
    The sweetness of the hay.

Now the weariest of all mothers,
    The saddest two years' bride,
She scowls in the face of her husband,
    And spurns her child aside.

"Rake out the red coals, goodman,—
    For there the child shall lie,
Till the black witch comes to fetch her
    And both up chimney fly.

"It's never my own little daughter,
 It's never my own," she said;
"The witches have stolen my Anna,
 And left me an imp instead.

"Oh, fair and sweet was my baby,
 Blue eyes, and hair of gold;
But this is ugly and wrinkled,
 Cross, and cunning, and old.

"I hate the touch of her fingers,
 I hate the feel of her skin;
It's not the milk from my bosom,
 But my blood, that she sucks in.

"My face grows sharp with the torment
 Look! my arms are skin and bone!
Rake open the red coals, goodman,
 And the witch shall have her own.

"She'll come when she hears it crying,
 In the shape of an owl or bat,
And she'll bring us our darling Anna
 In place of her screeching brat."

Then the goodman, Ezra Dalton,
 Laid his hand upon her head:
"Thy sorrow is great, O woman!
 I sorrow with thee," he said.

"The paths to trouble are many,
 And never but one sure way

THE CHANGELING

Leads out to the light beyond it:
  My poor wife, let us pray."

Then he said to the great All-Father,
  "Thy daughter is weak and blind;
Let her sight come back, and clothe her
  Once more in her right mind.

Lead her out of this evil shadow,
  Out of these fancies wild;
Let the holy love of the mother
  Turn again to her child.

Make her lips like the lips of Mary
  Kissing her blessed Son;
Let her hands, like the hands of Jesus,
  Rest on her little one.

Comfort the soul of thy handmaid,
  Open her prison-door,
And thine shall be all the glory
  And praise forevermore."

Then into the face of its mother
  The baby looked up and smiled;
And the cloud of her soul was lifted,
  And she knew her little child.

A beam of the slant west sunshine
  Made the wan face almost fair,
Lit the blue eyes' patient wonder
  And the rings of pale gold hair.

She kissed it on lip and forehead,
   She kissed it on cheek and chin,
And she bared her snow-white bosom
   To the lips so pale and thin.

Oh, fair on her bridal morning
   Was the maid who blushed and smiled
But fairer to Ezra Dalton
   Looked the mother of his child.

With more than a lover's fondness
   He stooped to her worn young face,
And the nursing child and the mother
   He folded in one embrace.

"Blessed be God!" he murmured.
   "Blessed be God!" she said;
"For I see, who once was blinded, —
   I live, who once was dead.

"Now mount and ride, my goodman,
   As thou lovest thy own soul!
Woe's me, if my wicked fancies
   Be the death of Goody Cole!"

His horse he saddled and bridled,
   And into the night rode he,
Now through the great black woodland,
   Now by the white-beached sea.

He rode through the silent clearings,
   He came to the ferry wide,

And thrice he called to the boatman
   Asleep on the other side.

He set his horse to the river,
   He swam to Newbury town,
And he called up Justice Sewall
   In his nightcap and his gown.

And the grave and worshipful justice
   (Upon whose soul be peace!)
Set his name to the jailer's warrant
   For Goodwife Cole's release.

Then through the night the hoof-beats
   Went sounding like a flail;
And Goody Cole at cockcrow
   Came forth from Ipswich jail.

"Here is a rhyme: I hardly dare
   To venture on its theme worn out;
What seems so sweet by Doon and Ayr
   Sounds simply silly hereabout;
And pipes by lips Arcadian blown
Are only tin horns at our own.
Yet still the muse of pastoral walks with us,
While Hosea Biglow sings, our new Theocritus."

THE MAIDS OF ATTITASH

Attitash, an Indian word signifying "huckleberry," is the name of a large and beautiful lake in the northern part of Amesbury. [In a letter to Mr. Fields, Whittier wrote: "I should like to show thee Attitash, as it is as pretty as St. Mary's Lake which Wordsworth sings, in fact a great deal prettier. The glimpse of the Pawtuckaway range of mountains in Nottingham seen across it is very fine, and it has noble groves of pines and maples and ash trees."]

In sky and wave the white clouds swam,
And the blue hills of Nottingham
  Through gaps of leafy green
  Across the lake were seen,

When, in the shadow of the ash
That dreams its dream in Attitash,
  In the warm summer weather,
  Two maidens sat together.

They sat and watched in idle mood
The gleam and shade of lake and wood;
  The beach the keen light smote,
  The white sail of a boat;

Swan flocks of lilies shoreward lying,
In sweetness, not in music, dying;
  Hardhack, and virgin's-bower,
  And white-spiked clethra-flower.

With careless ears they heard the plash
And breezy wash of Attitash,

The wood-bird's plaintive cry,
The locust's sharp reply.

And teased the while, with playful hand,
The shaggy dog of Newfoundland,
  Whose uncouth frolic spilled
  Their baskets berry-filled.

Then one, the beauty of whose eyes
Was evermore a great surprise,
  Tossed back her queenly head,
  And lightly laughing, said:

No bridegroom's hand be mine to hold
That is not lined with yellow gold;
  I tread no cottage-floor;
  I own no lover poor.

My love must come on silken wings,
With bridal lights of diamond rings,
  Not foul with kitchen smirch,
  With tallow-dip for torch."

The other, on whose modest head
Was lesser dower of beauty shed,
  With look for home-hearths meet,
  And voice exceeding sweet,

Answered, "We will not rivals be ;
Take thou the gold, leave love to me;
  Mine be the cottage small,
  And thine the rich man's hall.

"I know, indeed, that wealth is good;
But lowly roof and simple food,
  With love that hath no doubt,
  Are more than gold without."

Hard by a farmer hale and young
His cradle in the rye-field swung,
  Tracking the yellow plain
  With windrows of ripe grain.

And still, whene'er he paused to whet
His scythe, the sidelong glance he met
  Of large dark eyes, where strove
  False pride and secret love.

Be strong, young mower of the grain;
That love shall overmatch disdain,
  Its instincts soon or late
  The heart shall vindicate.

In blouse of gray, with fishing-rod,
Half screened by leaves, a stranger trod
  The margin of the pond,
  Watching the group beyond.

The supreme hours unnoted come;
Unfelt the turning tides of doom;
  And so the maids laughed on,
  Nor dreamed what fate had done, —

Nor knew the step was Destiny's
That rustled in the birchen trees.

As, with their lives forecast,
Fisher and mower passed.

Erelong by lake and rivulet side
The summer roses paled and died,
  And Autumn's fingers shed
  The maple's leaves of red.

Through the long gold-hazed afternoon,
Alone, but for the diving loon,
  The partridge in the brake,
  The black duck on the lake,

Beneath the shadow of the ash
Sat man and maid by Attitash;
  And earth and air made room
  For human hearts to bloom.

Soft spread the carpets of the sod,
And scarlet-oak and golden-rod
  With blushes and with smiles
  Lit up the forest aisles.

The mellow light the lake aslant,
The pebbled margin's ripple-chant
  Attempered and low-toned,
  The tender mystery owned.

And through the dream the lovers dreamed
Sweet sounds stole in and soft lights streamed;
  The sunshine seemed to bless,
  The air was a caress.

Not she who lightly laughed is there,
With scornful toss of midnight hair,
　Her dark, disdainful eyes,
　And proud lip worldly-wise.

Her haughty vow is still unsaid,
But all she dreamed and coveted
　Wears, half to her surprise,
　The youthful farmer's guise!

With more than all her old-time pride
She walks the rye-field at his side,
　Careless of cot or hall,
　Since love transfigures all.

Rich beyond dreams, the vantage-ground
Of life is gained; her hands have found
　The talisman of old
　That changes all to gold.

While she who could for love dispense
With all its glittering accidents,
　And trust her heart alone,
　Finds love and gold her own.

What wealth can buy or art can build
Awaits her; but her cup is filled
　Even now unto the brim;
　Her world is love and him!

The while he heard, the Book-man drew
   A length of make-believing face,
With smothered mischief laughing through:
   " Why, you shall sit in Ramsay's place,
And, with his Gentle Shepherd, keep
On Yankee hills immortal sheep,
While love-lorn swains and maids the seas beyond
Hold dreamy tryst around your huckleberry-pond."

The Traveller laughed: " Sir Galahad
   Singing of love the Trouvere's lay!
How should he know the blindfold lad
   From one of Vulcan's forge-boys?" — " Nay,
He better sees who stands outside
Than they who in procession ride,"
The reader answered: " selectmen and squire
Miss, while they make, the show that wayside folks admire.

" Here is a wild tale of the North,
   Our travelled friend will own as one
Fit for a Norland Christmas hearth
   And lips of Christian Andersen.
They tell it in the valleys green
Of the fair island he has seen,
Low lying off the pleasant Swedish shore,
Washed by the Baltic Sea, and watched by Elsinore."

KALLUNDBORG CHURCH

> "Tie stille, barn min !
> Imorgen kommer Fin,
> Fa'er din,
> Og gi'er dig Esbern Snares öine og hjerte at lege med
> *Zealand Rhyme*

"Build at Kallundborg by the sea
A church as stately as church may be,
And there thou shalt wed my daughter fair,"
Said the Lord of Nesvek to Esbern Snare.

And the Baron laughed. But Esbern said,
"Though I lose my soul, I will Helva wed!"
And off he strode, in his pride of will,
To the Troll who dwelt in Ulshoi hill.

"Build, O Troll, a church for me
At Kallundborg by the mighty sea;
Build it stately, and build it fair,
Build it quickly," said Esbern Snare.

But the sly Dwarf said, "No work is wrought
By Trolls of the Hills, O man, for naught.
What wilt thou give for thy church so fair?"
"Set thy own price," quoth Esbern Snare.

"When Kallundborg church is builded well,
Thou must the name of its builder tell,
Or thy heart and thy eyes must be my boon."
"Build," said Esbern, "and build it soon."

KALLUNDBORG CHURCH

By night and by day the Troll wrought on;
He hewed the timbers, he piled the stone;
But day by day, as the walls rose fair,
Darker and sadder grew Esbern Snare.

He listened by night, he watched by day,
He sought and thought, but he dared not pray;
In vain he called on the Elle-maids shy,
And the Neck and the Nis gave no reply.

Of his evil bargain far and wide
A rumor ran through the country-side;
And Helva of Nesvek, young and fair,
Prayed for the soul of Esbern Snare.

And now the church was wellnigh done;
One pillar it lacked, and one alone;
And the grim Troll muttered, "Fool thou art!
To-morrow gives me thy eyes and heart!"

By Kallundborg in black despair,
Through wood and meadow, walked Esbern Snare,
Till, worn and weary, the strong man sank
Under the birches on Ulshoi bank.

At his last day's work he heard the Troll
Hammer and delve in the quarry's hole;
Before him the church stood large and fair:
I have builded my tomb," said Esbern Snare.

And he closed his eyes the sight to hide,
When he heard a light step at his side:

"O Esbern Snare!" a sweet voice said,
"Would I might die now in thy stead!"

With a grasp by love and by fear made strong,
He held her fast, and he held her long;
With the beating heart of a bird afeard,
She hid her face in his flame-red beard.

"O love!" he cried, "let me look to-day
In thine eyes ere mine are plucked away;
Let me hold thee close, let them feel thy heart
Ere mine by the Troll is torn apart!

"I sinned, O Helva, for love of thee!
Pray that the Lord Christ pardon me!"
But fast as she prayed, and faster still,
Hammered the Troll in Ulshoi hill.

He knew, as he wrought, that a loving heart
Was somehow baffling his evil art;
For more than spell of Elf or Troll
Is a maiden's prayer for her lover's soul.

And Esbern listened, and caught the sound
Of a Troll-wife singing underground:
"To-morrow comes Fine, father thine:
Lie still and hush thee, baby mine!

"Lie still, my darling! next sunrise
Thou 'lt play with Esbern Snare's heart and
    eyes!"
"Ho! ho!" quoth Esbern, "is that your game?
Thanks to the Troll-wife, I know his name!"

The Troll he heard him, and hurried on
To Kallundborg church with the lacking stone.
"Too late, Gaffer Fine!" cried Esbern Snare;
And Troll and pillar vanished in air!

That night the harvesters heard the sound
Of a woman sobbing underground,
And the voice of the Hill-Troll loud with blame
Of the careless singer who told his name.

Of the Troll of the Church they sing the rune
By the Northern Sea in the harvest moon;
And the fishers of Zealand hear him still
Scolding his wife in Ulshoi hill.

And seaward over its groves of birch
Still looks the tower of Kallundborg church,
Where, first at its altar, a wedded pair,
Stood Helva of Nesvek and Esbern Snare!

"What," asked the Traveller, "would our sires,
  The old Norse story-tellers, say
Of sun-graved pictures, ocean wires,
  And smoking steamboats of to-day?
And this, O lady, by your leave,
Recalls your song of yester eve:
Pray, let us have that Cable-hymn once more."
"Hear, hear!" the Book-man cried, "the lady has
  the floor.

"These noisy waves below perhaps
  To such a strain will lend their ear,
With softer voice and lighter lapse
  Come stealing up the sands to hear,
And what they once refused to do
  For old King Knut accord to you.
Nay, even the fishes shall your listeners be,
As once, the legend runs, they heard St. Anthony

THE CABLE HYMN

O LONELY bay of Trinity,
  O dreary shores, give ear!
Lean down unto the white-lipped sea,
  The voice of God to hear!

From world to world His couriers fly,
  Thought-winged and shod with fire;
The angel of His stormy sky
  Rides down the sunken wire.

What saith the herald of the Lord?
  "The world's long strife is done;
Close wedded by that mystic cord,
  Its continents are one.

"And one in heart, as one in blood,
  Shall all her peoples be;
The hands of human brotherhood
  Are clasped beneath the sea.

"Through Orient seas, o'er Afric's plain
  And Asian mountains borne.

THE CABLE HYMN

The vigor of the Northern brain
   Shall nerve the world outworn.

From clime to clime, from shore to shore,
   Shall thrill the magic thread;
The new Prometheus steals once more
   The fire that wakes the dead."

Throb on, strong pulse of thunder! beat
   From answering beach to beach;
Fuse nations in thy kindly heat,
   And melt the chains of each!

Wild terror of the sky above,
   Glide tamed and dumb below!
Bear gently, Ocean's carrier-dove,
   Thy errands to and fro.

Weave on, swift shuttle of the Lord,
   Beneath the deep so far,
The bridal robe of earth's accord,
   The funeral shroud of war!

For lo! the fall of Ocean's wall
   Space mocked and time outrun;
And round the world the thought of all
   Is as the thought of one!

The poles unite, the zones agree,
   The tongues of striving cease;
As on the Sea of Galilee
   The Christ is whispering, Peace!

"Glad prophecy! to this at last,"
  The Reader said, "shall all things come.
Forgotten be the bugle's blast,
  And battle-music of the drum.
A little while the world may run
Its old mad way, with needle-gun
And ironclad, but truth, at last, shall reign:
The cradle-song of Christ was never sung in vain!"

Shifting his scattered papers, "Here,"
  He said, as died the faint applause,
"Is something that I found last year
  Down on the island known as Orr's.
I had it from a fair-haired girl
Who, oddly, bore the name of Pearl,
(As if by some droll freak of circumstance,)
Classic, or wellnigh so, in Harriet Stowe's romance."

THE DEAD SHIP OF HARPSWELL

What flecks the outer gray beyond
  The sundown's golden trail?
The white flash of a sea-bird's wing,
  Or gleam of slanting sail?
Let young eyes watch from Neck and Point,
  And sea-worn elders pray, —
The ghost of what was once a ship
  Is sailing up the bay!

From gray sea-fog, from icy drift,
  From peril and from pain,

THE DEAD SHIP OF HARPSWELL

The home-bound fisher greets thy lights,
    O hundred-harbored Maine!
But many a keel shall seaward turn,
    And many a sail outstand,
When, tall and white, the Dead Ship looms
    Against the dusk of land.

She rounds the headland's bristling pines;
    She threads the isle-set bay;
No spur of breeze can speed her on,
    Nor ebb of tide delay.
Old men still walk the Isle of Orr
    Who tell her date and name,
Old shipwrights sit in Freeport yards
    Who hewed her oaken frame.

What weary doom of baffled quest,
    Thou sad sea-ghost, is thine?
What makes thee in the haunts of home
    A wonder and a sign?
No foot is on thy silent deck,
    Upon thy helm no hand;
No ripple hath the soundless wind
    That smites thee from the land!

For never comes the ship to port,
    Howe'er the breeze may be;
Just when she nears the waiting shore
    She drifts again to sea.
No tack of sail, nor turn of helm,
    Nor sheer of veering side;
Stern-fore she drives to sea and night,
    Against the wind and tide.

In vain o'er Harpswell Neck the star
  Of evening guides her in;
In vain for her the lamps are lit
  Within thy tower, Seguin!
In vain the harbor-boat shall hail,
  In vain the pilot call;
No hand shall reef her spectral sail,
  Or let her anchor fall.

Shake, brown old wives, with dreary joy,
  Your gray-head hints of ill;
And, over sick-beds whispering low,
  Your prophecies fulfil.
Some home amid yon birchen trees
  Shall drape its door with woe;
And slowly where the Dead Ship sails,
  The burial boat shall row!

From Wolf Neck and from Flying Point
  From island and from main,
From sheltered cove and tided creek,
  Shall glide the funeral train.
The dead-boat with the bearers four,
  The mourners at her stern, —
And one shall go the silent way
  Who shall no more return!

And men shall sigh, and women weep,
  Whose dear ones pale and pine,
And sadly over sunset seas
  Await the ghostly sign.

They know not that its sails are filled
  By pity's tender breath,
Nor see the Angel at the helm
  Who steers the Ship of Death!

"Chill as a down-east breeze should be,"
  The Book-man said. "A ghostly touch
The legend has. I'm glad to see
  Your flying Yankee beat the Dutch."
"Well, here is something of the sort
  Which one midsummer day I caught
In Narragansett Bay, for lack of fish."
"We wait," the Traveller said; "serve hot or cold
  your dish."

THE PALATINE

Block Island in Long Island Sound, called by the Indians Manisees, the isle of the little god, was the scene of a tragic incident a hundred years or more ago, when *The Palatine*, an emigrant ship bound for Philadelphia, driven off its course, came upon the coast at this point. A mutiny on board, followed by an inhuman desertion on the part of the crew, had brought the unhappy passengers to the verge of starvation and madness. Tradition says that wreckers on shore, after rescuing all but one of the survivors, set fire to the vessel, which was driven out to sea before a gale which had sprung up. Every twelvemonth, according to the same tradition, the spectacle of a ship on fire is visible to the inhabitants of the island.

LEAGUES north, as fly the gull and auk,
Point Judith watches with eye of hawk;
Leagues south, thy beacon flames, Montauk!

Lonely and wind-shorn, wood-forsaken,
With never a tree for Spring to waken,
For tryst of lovers or farewells taken,

Circled by waters that never freeze,
Beaten by billow and swept by breeze,
Lieth the island of Manisees,

Set at the mouth of the Sound to hold
The coast lights up on its turret old,
Yellow with moss and sea-fog mould.

Dreary the land when gust and sleet
At its doors and windows howl and beat,
And Winter laughs at its fires of peat!

But in summer time, when pool and pond,
Held in the laps of valleys fond,
Are blue as the glimpses of sea beyond;

When the hills are sweet with the brier-rose,
And, hid in the warm, soft dells, unclose
Flowers the mainland rarely knows;

When boats to their morning fishing go,
And, held to the wind and slanting low,
Whitening and darkening the small sails show —

Then is that lonely island fair;
And the pale health-seeker findeth there
The wine of life in its pleasant air.

THE PALATINE

No greener valleys the sun invite,
On smoother beaches no sea-birds light,
No blue waves shatter to foam more white!

There, circling ever their narrow range,
Quaint tradition and legend strange
Live on unchallenged, and know no change.

Old wives spinning their web of tow,
Or rocking weirdly to and fro
In and out of the peat's dull glow,

And old men mending their nets of twine,
Talk together of dream and sign,
Talk of the lost ship Palatine, —

The ship that, a hundred years before,
Freighted deep with its goodly store,
In the gales of the equinox went ashore.

The eager islanders one by one
Counted the shots of her signal gun,
And heard the crash when she drove right on!

Into the teeth of death she sped:
(May God forgive the hands that fed
The false lights over the rocky Head!)

O men and brothers! what sights were there!
White upturned faces, hands stretched in prayer!
Where waves had pity, could ye not spare?

Down swooped the wreckers, like birds of prey
Tearing the heart of the ship away,
And the dead had never a word to say.

And then, with ghastly shimmer and shine
Over the rocks and the seething brine,
They burned the wreck of the Palatine.

In their cruel hearts, as they homeward sped,
"The sea and the rocks are dumb," they said:
"There 'll be no reckoning with the dead."

But the year went round, and when once more
Along their foam-white curves of shore
They heard the line-storm rave and roar,

Behold! again, with shimmer and shine,
Over the rocks and the seething brine,
The flaming wreck of the Palatine!

So, haply in fitter words than these,
Mending their nets on their patient knees,
They tell the legend of Manisees.

Nor looks nor tones a doubt betray;
"It is known to us all," they quietly say;
"We too have seen it in our day."

Is there, then, no death for a word once spoken?
Was never a deed but left its token
Written on tables never broken?

Do the elements subtle reflections give?
Do pictures of all the ages live
On Nature's infinite negative,

Which, half in sport, in malice half,
She shows at times, with shudder or laugh,
Phantom and shadow in photograph?

For still, on many a moonless night,
From Kingston Head and from Montauk light
The spectre kindles and burns in sight.

Now low and dim, now clear and higher,
Leaps up the terrible Ghost of Fire,
Then, slowly sinking, the flames expire.

And the wise Sound skippers, though skies be fine,
Reef their sails when they see the sign
Of the blazing wreck of the Palatine!

———

"A fitter tale to scream than sing,"
　　The Book-man said. "Well, fancy, then,"
　The Reader answered, "on the wing
　　The sea-birds shriek it, not for men,
　But in the ear of wave and breeze!"
　The Traveller mused: "Your Manisees
Is fairy-land: off Narragansett shore
Who ever saw the isle or heard its name before?

"'T is some strange land of Flyaway,
　Whose dreamy shore the ship beguiles,

St. Brandan's in its sea-mist gray,
　Or sunset loom of Fortunate Isles!"
"No ghost, but solid turf and rock
　Is the good island known as Block,"
The Reader said. "For beauty and for ease
I chose its Indian name, soft-flowing Manisees!

"But let it pass; here is a bit
　Of unrhymed story, with a hint
Of the old preaching mood in it,
　The sort of sidelong moral squint
Our friend objects to, which has grown,
I fear, a habit of my own.
'T was written when the Asian plague drew near,
And the land held its breath and paled with sudden fear."

ABRAHAM DAVENPORT

The famous Dark Day of New England, May 19, 1780, was a physical puzzle for many years to our ancestors, but its occurrence brought something more than philosophical speculation into the minds of those who passed through it. The incident of Colonel Abraham Davenport's sturdy protest is a matter of history.

IN the old days (a custom laid aside
With breeches and cocked hats) the people sent
Their wisest men to make the public laws.
And so, from a brown homestead, where the Sound
Drinks the small tribute of the Mianas,

ABRAHAM DAVENPORT

Waved over by the woods of Rippowams,
And hallowed by pure lives and tranquil deaths,
Stamford sent up to the councils of the State
Wisdom and grace in Abraham Davenport.

'T was on a May-day of the far old year
Seventeen hundred eighty, that there fell
Over the bloom and sweet life of the Spring,
Over the fresh earth and the heaven of noon,
A horror of great darkness, like the night
In day of which the Norland sagas tell, —
The Twilight of the Gods. The low-hung sky
Was black with ominous clouds, save where its rim
Was fringed with a dull glow, like that which
    climbs
The crater's sides from the red hell below.
Birds ceased to sing, and all the barn-yard fowls
Roosted; the cattle at the pasture bars
Lowed, and looked homeward; bats on leathern
    wings
Flitted abroad; the sounds of labor died;
Men prayed, and women wept; all ears grew
    sharp
To hear the doom-blast of the trumpet shatter
The black sky, that the dreadful face of Christ
Might look from the rent clouds, not as he looked
A loving guest at Bethany, but stern
As Justice and inexorable Law.

   Meanwhile in the old State House, dim as
    ghosts,
Sat the lawgivers of Connecticut,

Trembling beneath their legislative robes.
"It is the Lord's Great Day! Let us adjourn,"
Some said; and then, as if with one accord,
All eyes were turned to Abraham Davenport.
He rose, slow cleaving with his steady voice
The intolerable hush. "This well may be
The Day of Judgment which the world awaits;
But be it so or not, I only know
My present duty, and my Lord's command
To occupy till He come. So at the post
Where He hath set me in His providence,
I choose, for one, to meet Him face to face, —
No faithless servant frightened from my task,
But ready when the Lord of the harvest calls;
And therefore, with all reverence, I would say,
Let God do His work, we will see to ours.
Bring in the candles." And they brought them
 in.

Then by the flaring lights the Speaker read,
Albeit with husky voice and shaking hands,
An act to amend an act to regulate
The shad and alewive fisheries. Whereupon
Wisely and well spake Abraham Davenport,
Straight to the question, with no figures of speech
Save the ten Arab signs, yet not without
The shrewd dry humor natural to the man:
His awe-struck colleagues listening all the while,
Between the pauses of his argument,
To hear the thunder of the wrath of God
Break from the hollow trumpet of the cloud.

And there he stands in memory to this day,
Erect, self-poised, a rugged face, half seen
Against the background of unnatural dark,
A witness to the ages as they pass,
That simple duty hath no place for fear.

He ceased: just then the ocean seemed
    To lift a half-faced moon in sight;
And, shore-ward, o'er the waters gleamed,
    From crest to crest, a line of light,
Such as of old, with solemn awe,
The fishers by Gennesaret saw,
When dry-shod o'er it walked the Son of God,
Tracking the waves with light where'er his sandals trod.

Silently for a space each eye
    Upon that sudden glory turned:
Cool from the land the breeze blew by,
    The tent-ropes flapped, the long beach churned
Its waves to foam; on either hand
Stretched, far as sight, the hills of sand;
With bays of marsh, and capes of bush and tree,
The wood's black shore-line loomed beyond the meadowy sea.

The lady rose to leave. "One song,
    Or hymn," they urged, "before we part."
And she, with lips to which belong
    Sweet intuitions of all art.

Gave to the winds of night a strain
Which they who heard would hear again;
And to her voice the solemn ocean lent,
Touching its harp of sand, a deep accompaniment

THE WORSHIP OF NATURE

The harp at Nature's advent strung
   Has never ceased to play;
The song the stars of morning sung
   Has never died away.

And prayer is made, and praise is given,
   By all things near and far;
The ocean looketh up to heaven,
   And mirrors every star.

Its waves are kneeling on the strand,
   As kneels the human knee,
Their white locks bowing to the sand,
   The priesthood of the sea!

They pour their glittering treasures forth,
   Their gifts of pearl they bring,
And all the listening hills of earth
   Take up the song they sing.

The green earth sends her incense up
   From many a mountain shrine;
From folded leaf and dewy cup
   She pours her sacred wine.

THE WORSHIP OF NATURE

The mists above the morning rills
  Rise white as wings of prayer;
The altar-curtains of the hills
  Are sunset's purple air.

The winds with hymns of praise are loud,
  Or low with sobs of pain, —
The thunder-organ of the cloud,
  The dropping tears of rain.

With drooping head and branches crossed
  The twilight forest grieves,
Or speaks with tongues of Pentecost
  From all its sunlit leaves.

The blue sky is the temple's arch,
  Its transept earth and air,
The music of its starry march
  The chorus of a prayer.

So Nature keeps the reverent frame
  With which her years began,
And all her signs and voices shame
  The prayerless heart of man.

The singer ceased. The moon's white rays
  Fell on the rapt, still face of her.
Allah il Allah! He hath praise
  From all things," said the Traveller.
Oft from the desert's silent nights,
  And mountain hymns of sunset lights,

My heart has felt rebuke, as in his tent
The Moslem's prayer has shamed my Christian
    knee unbent."

He paused, and lo! far, faint, and slow
  The bells in Newbury's steeples tolled
The twelve dead hours; the lamp burned low;
  The singer sought her canvas fold.
One sadly said, "At break of day
  We strike our tent and go our way."
But one made answer cheerily, "Never fear,
We 'll pitch this tent of ours in type another year."

EGO

WRITTEN IN THE ALBUM OF A FRIEND

ON page of thine I cannot trace
  The cold and heartless commonplace,
A statue's fixed and marble grace.

For ever as these lines I penned,
Still with the thought of thee will blend
That of some loved and common friend,

Who in life's desert track has made
His pilgrim tent with mine, or strayed
Beneath the same remembered shade.

And hence my pen unfettered moves
In freedom which the heart approves,
The negligence which friendship loves.

And wilt thou prize my poor gift less
For simple air and rustic dress,
And sign of haste and carelessness?

Oh, more than specious counterfeit
Of sentiment or studied wit,
A heart like thine should value it.

Yet half I fear my gift will be
Unto thy book, if not to thee,
Of more than doubtful courtesy.

A banished name from Fashion's sphere,
A lay unheard of Beauty's ear,
Forbid, disowned, — what do they here?

Upon my ear not all in vain
Came the sad captive's clanking chain,
The groaning from his bed of pain.

And sadder still, I saw the woe
Which only wounded spirits know
When Pride's strong footsteps o'er them go.

Spurned not alone in walks abroad,
But from the temples of the Lord
Thrust out apart, like things abhorred.

Deep as I felt, and stern and strong,
In words which Prudence smothered long,
My soul spoke out against the wrong;

EGO

Not mine alone the task to speak
Of comfort to the poor and weak,
And dry the tear on Sorrow's cheek;

But, mingled in the conflict warm,
To pour the fiery breath of storm
Through the harsh trumpet of Reform;

To brave Opinion's settled frown,
From ermined robe and saintly gown,
While wrestling reverenced Error down.

Founts gushed beside my pilgrim way,
Cool shadows on the greensward lay,
Flowers swung upon the bending spray.

And, broad and bright, on either hand,
Stretched the green slopes of Fairy-land,
With Hope's eternal sunbow spanned;

Whence voices called me like the flow,
Which on the listener's ear will grow,
Of forest streamlets soft and low.

And gentle eyes, which still retain
Their picture on the heart and brain,
Smiled, beckoning from that path of pain

In vain! nor dream, nor rest, nor pause
Remain for him who round him draws
The battered mail of Freedom's cause.

EGO

From youthful hopes, from each green spot
Of young Romance, and gentle Thought,
Where storm and tumult enter not;

From each fair altar, where belong
The offerings Love requires of Song
In homage to her bright-eyed throng;

With soul and strength, with heart and hand,
I turned to Freedom's struggling band,
To the sad Helots of our land.

What marvel then that Fame should turn
Her notes of praise to those of scorn;
Her gifts reclaimed, her smiles withdrawn?

What matters it? a few years more,
Life's surge so restless heretofore
Shall break upon the unknown shore!

In that far land shall disappear
The shadows which we follow here,
The mist-wreaths of our atmosphere!

Before no work of mortal hand,
Of human will or strength expand
The pearl gates of the Better Land;

Alone in that great love which gave
Life to the sleeper of the grave,
Resteth the power to seek and save.

Yet, if the spirit gazing through
The vista of the past can view
One deed to Heaven and virtue true;

If through the wreck of wasted powers,
Of garlands wreathed from Folly's bowers
Of idle aims and misspent hours,

The eye can note one sacred spot
By Pride and Self profanèd not,
A green place in the waste of thought,

Where deed or word hath rendered less
The sum of human wretchedness,
And Gratitude looks forth to bless;

The simple burst of tenderest feeling
From sad hearts worn by evil-dealing,
For blessing on the hand of healing;

Better than Glory's pomp will be
That green and blessed spot to me,
A palm-shade in Eternity!

Something of Time which may invite
The purified and spiritual sight
To rest on with a calm delight.

And when the summer winds shall sweep
With their light wings my place of sleep,
And mosses round my headstone creep;

If still, as Freedom's rallying sign,
Upon the young heart's altars shine
The very fires they caught from mine;

If words my lips once uttered still,
In the calm faith and steadfast will
Of other hearts, their work fulfil;

Perchance with joy the soul may learn
These tokens, and its eye discern
The fires which on those altars burn;

A marvellous joy that even then,
The spirit hath its life again,
In the strong hearts of mortal men.

Take, lady, then, the gift I bring,
No gay and graceful offering,
No flower-smile of the laughing spring.

Midst the green buds of Youth's fresh May,
With Fancy's leaf-enwoven bay,
My sad and sombre gift I lay.

And if it deepens in thy mind
A sense of suffering human-kind,—
The outcast and the spirit-blind;

Oppressed and spoiled on every side,
By Prejudice, and Scorn, and Pride,
Life's common courtesies denied:

Sad mothers mourning o'er their trust,
Children by want and misery nursed,
Tasting life's bitter cup at first;

If to their strong appeals which come
From fireless hearth, and crowded room,
And the close alley's noisome gloom, —

Though dark the hands upraised to thee
In mute beseeching agony,
Thou lend'st thy woman's sympathy;

Not vainly on thy gentle shrine,
Where Love, and Mirth, and Friendship twine
Their varied gifts, I offer mine.

MY PSALM

I MOURN no more my vanished years:
   Beneath a tender rain,
An April rain of smiles and tears,
   My heart is young again.

The west-winds blow, and, singing low,
   I hear the glad streams run;
The windows of my soul I throw
   Wide open to the sun.

No longer forward nor behind
   I look in hope or fear;
But, grateful, take the good I find,
   The best of now and here.

MY PSALM

I plough no more a desert land,
    To harvest weed and tare;
The manna dropping from God's hand
    Rebukes my painful care.

I break my pilgrim staff, I lay
    Aside the toiling oar;
The angel sought so far away
    I welcome at my door.

The airs of spring may never play
    Among the ripening corn,
Nor freshness of the flowers of May
    Blow through the autumn morn;

Yet shall the blue-eyed gentian look
    Through fringèd lids to heaven,
And the pale aster in the brook
    Shall see its image given;—

The woods shall wear their robes of praise,
    The south-wind softly sigh,
And sweet, calm days in golden haze
    Melt down the amber sky.

Not less shall manly deed and word
    Rebuke an age of wrong;
The graven flowers that wreathe the sword
    Make not the blade less strong.

But smiting hands shall learn to heal,—
    To build as to destroy;

Nor less my heart for others feel
    That I the more enjoy.

All as God wills, who wisely heeds
    To give or to withhold,
And knoweth more of all my needs
    Than all my prayers have told!

Enough that blessings undeserved
    Have marked my erring track;
That wheresoe'er my feet have swerved
    His chastening turned me back;

That more and more a Providence
    Of love is understood,
Making the springs of time and sense
    Sweet with eternal good; —

That death seems but a covered way
    Which opens into light,
Wherein no blinded child can stray
    Beyond the Father's sight;

That care and trial seem at last,
    Through Memory's sunset air,
Like mountain-ranges overpast,
    In purple distance fair;

That all the jarring notes of life
    Seem blending in a psalm,
And all the angles of its strife
    Slow rounding into calm.

And so the shadows fall apart,
    And so the west-winds play;
    And all the windows of my heart
    I open to the day.

RESPONSE

On the occasion of my seventieth birthday, in 1877, I was the recipient of many tokens of esteem. The publishers of the *Atlantic Monthly* gave a dinner in my name, and the editor of *The Literary World* gathered in his paper many affectionate messages from my associates in literature and the cause of human progress. The lines which follow were written in acknowledgment.

BESIDE that milestone where the level sun,
    Nigh unto setting, sheds his last, low rays
On word and work irrevocably done,
Life's blending threads of good and ill outspun,
    I hear, O friends! your words of cheer and praise,
Half doubtful if myself or otherwise.
    Like him who, in the old Arabian joke,
A beggar slept and crownèd Caliph woke.
Thanks not the less. With not unglad surprise
I see my life-work through your partial eyes;
Assured, in giving to my home-taught songs
A higher value than of right belongs,
You do but read between the written lines
The finer grace of unfulfilled designs.

AT LAST

[Recited by one of the little group of relations, who stood by the poet's bedside, as the last moment of his life approached.]

WHEN on my day of life the night is falling,
    And, in the winds from unsunned spaces blown,
I hear far voices out of darkness calling
    My feet to paths unknown,

Thou who hast made my home of life so pleasant,
    Leave not its tenant when its walls decay;
O Love Divine, O Helper ever present,
    Be Thou my strength and stay!

Be near me when all else is from me drifting;
    Earth, sky, home's pictures, days of shade and shine,
And kindly faces to my own uplifting
    The love which answers mine.

I have but Thee, my Father! let Thy spirit
    Be with me then to comfort and uphold;
No gate of pearl, no branch of palm I merit,
    Nor street of shining gold.

Suffice it if — my good and ill unreckoned,
    And both forgiven through Thy abounding grace —
I find myself by hands familiar beckoned
    Unto my fitting place.

Some humble door among Thy many mansions,
  Some sheltering shade where sin and striving cease,
And flows forever through heaven's green expansions
  The river of Thy peace.

There, from the music round about me stealing,
  I fain would learn the new and holy song,
And find at last, beneath Thy trees of healing,
  The life for which I long.

NOTES

NOTES

Page 11, line 25. *Ah, brother! only I and thou.*
Matthew Franklin Whittier, born July 4, 1812, died January 7, 1883. In middle life, during his residence in Portland, he took a deep interest in the anti-slavery movement, and wrote a series of caustic letters under the signature Ethan Spike of Hornby.

Page 12, line 25. *The Chief of Gambia's golden shore.*
The African Chief was the title of a poem by Mrs. Sarah Wentworth Morton, wife of the Hon. Perez Morton, a former attorney-general of Massachusetts. Mrs. Morton's *nom de plume* was *Philenia*. The schoolbook in which *The African Chief* was printed was Caleb Bingham's *The American Preceptor*, and the poem contained fifteen stanzas, of which the first four were as follows : —

> See how the black ship cleaves the main
> High-bounding o'er the violet wave,
> Remurmuring with the groans of pain,
> Deep freighted with the princely slave.

> Did all the gods of Afric sleep,
> Forgetful of their guardian love,
> When the white traitors of the deep
> Betrayed him in the palmy grove?

> A chief of Gambia's golden shore,
> Whose arm the band of warriors led,
> Perhaps the lord of boundless power,
> By whom the foodless poor were fed.

> Does not the voice of reason cry,
> "Claim the first right which nature gave ;
> From the red scourge of bondage fly,
> Nor deign to live a burdened slave"?

Page 15, line 3. *From painful Sewel's ancient tome.*

William Sewel was the historian of the Quakers. Charles Lamb seemed to have as good an opinion of the book as Whittier. In his essay, *A Quakers' Meeting*, in *Essays of Elia*, he says : " Reader, if you are not acquainted with it, I would recommend to you, above all church-narratives, to read Sewel's *History of the Quakers*. . . . It is far more edifying and affecting than anything you will read of Wesley or his colleagues."

Page 15, line 6. *Or Chalkley's Journal, old and quaint.*

Thomas Chalkley was an Englishman of Quaker parentage, born in 1675, who travelled extensively as a preacher, and finally made his home in Philadelphia. He died in 1749 ; his *Journal* was first published in 1747. His own narrative of the incident which the poet relates is as follows : "To stop their murmuring, I told them they should not need to cast lots, which was usual in such cases, which of us should die first, for I would freely offer up my life to do them good. One said, 'God bless you ! I will not eat any of you.' Another said, 'He would die before he would eat any of me ;' and so said several. I can truly say, on that occasion, at that time, my life was not dear to me, and that I was serious and ingenuous in my proposition ; and as I was leaning over the side of the vessel, thoughtfully considering my proposal to the company, and looking in my mind to Him that made me, a very large dolphin came up towards the top or surface of the water, and looked me in the face ; and I called the people to put a hook into the sea, and take him, for here is one come to redeem me (I said to them). And they put a hook into the sea, and the fish readily took it, and they caught him. He was longer than myself. I think he was about six feet long, and the largest that ever I saw. This plainly showed us that we ought not to distrust the providence of the Almighty. The people were quieted by this act of Providence, and murmured no more. We caught enough to eat plentifully of, till we got into the capes of Delaware."

NOTES

Page 15, line 24. *Our uncle, innocent of books.*

For further account of Whittier's uncle Moses, the reader is referred to Whittier's *Prose Works*, volume I. p. 323.

Page 18, line 1. *There, too, our elder sister plied.*

Mary Whittier, born September 3, 1806, married Jacob Caldwell of Haverhill, had two children, Lewis Henry and Mary Elizabeth, and died January 7, 1860.

Page 18, line 19. *Our youngest and our dearest sat.*

Elizabeth Hussey Whittier, born December 7, 1815, was to her brother John what Dorothy Wordsworth was to William. It was her brother's opinion that "had her health, sense of duty, and almost morbid dread of spiritual and intellectual egotism permitted, she might have taken a high place among lyrical singers." She died September 3, 1864.

Page 19, line 31. *The master of the district school.*

Until near the end of his life, Whittier was unable to recall the name of the schoolmaster who stood for this figure in *Snow-Bound*. At last he remembered his name as Haskell, and from this clue the person was traced. He was George Haskell from Waterford, Maine, a Dartmouth student, who studied medicine, and removed to Illinois, where he was active in founding Shurtleff College. Later, he made his home at Vineland, New Jersey, where he aided in laying out the model community there, and especially in establishing an industrial school. He died in 1876, and seems never to have known that his portrait was drawn in *Snow-Bound*.

Page 22, line 7. *Another guest that winter night.*

In his introductory note, Whittier adds somewhat to his characterization of Harriet Livermore. At the time when *Snow-Bound* was written he did not know that she was living, or he might not have introduced her. She died in 1867.

Page 23, line 21. *The crazy Queen of Lebanon.*

An interesting account of Lady Hester Stanhope may be found in Kinglake's *Eothen*, chap. viii.

Page 27, line 3. *The wise old doctor* was Dr. Weld of Haverhill, an able man, who died at the age of ninety-six.

NOTES

Page 27, line 27. *Where Ellwood's meek, drab-skirted Muse.*

Thomas Ellwood, one of the Society of Friends, a contemporary and friend of Milton, and the suggester of *Paradise Regained*, wrote an epic poem in five books called *Davideis*, the life of King David of Israel. He wrote the book, we are told, for his own diversion, so it was not necessary that others should be diverted by it. Ellwood's autobiography, a quaint and delightful book, may be found in Howells's series of *Choice Autobiographies*.

Page 28, line 5. *Before us passed the painted Creeks.*

Referring to the removal of the Creek Indians from Georgia to beyond the Mississippi.

Page 28, line 6. *And daft McGregor on his raids.*

In 1822 Sir Gregor McGregor, a Scotchman, began an ineffectual attempt to establish a colony in Costa Rica.

Page 29, line 28. *These Flemish pictures of old days.*

In 1888 Whittier wrote the following lines on the fly-leaf of a copy of the first edition of *Snow-Bound*: —

>Twenty years have taken flight
>Since these pages saw the light.
> All home loves are gone,
>But not all with sadness, still,
>Do the eyes of memory fill
> As I gaze thereon.
>
>Lone and weary life seemed when
>First these pictures of the pen
> Grew upon my page;
>But I still have loving friends
>And the peace our Father sends
> Cheers the heart of age.

Page 35, line 7.

>*And the good man's voice, at strife*
>*With his shrill and tipsy wife.*

When Whittier first went to school with his sister Mary, the school-house was undergoing repairs, and the school was held in a dwelling-house, the other part of which was occupied by a tipsy and quarrelsome couple.

Page 48, line 1. *Here is the place ; right over the hill.*

"The place Whittier had in mind was his birthplace. There were beehives on the garden terrace near the well sweep, occupied perhaps by the descendants of Thomas Whittier's bees. The approach to the house from over the northern shoulder of Job's Hill by a path that was in constant use in his boyhood and still in existence, is accurately described in the poem. The 'gap in the old wall' is still to be seen, and 'the stepping stones in the shallow brook' are still in use. His sister's garden was down by the brookside in front of the house, and her daffodils are perpetuated and may now be found in their season each year in that place. The red-barred gate, the poplars, the cattle yard with 'the white horns tossing above the wall,' were all part of Whittier's boy life on the old farm. Even the touch of 'the sundown's blaze on her window pane' is realistic. The only place from which the blaze of the setting sun could be seen reflected in the windows of the old mansion is from the path so perfectly described. . . . All the story about Mary and her lover is wholly imaginative." S. T. PICKARD in his *Life and Letters of John Greenleaf Whittier.*

Page 76, line 13. *I see the gray fort's broken wall.*

The place that was in the mind of the poet when he wrote this stanza was on the rocks at Marblehead, where he had spent an early morning more than forty years before.

Page 102, line 16. *He loved himself the singer's art.*

Mr. Fields printed privately a volume of verse which called out Mr. Whittier's pleasant lines *To James T. Fields on a blank leaf of* "*Poems printed not published.*" Another poem *In Memory* was written after the death of his publisher and friend.

Page 102, line 23.
Pleasant it was to roam about
The lettered world as he had done.

Mr. Fields's *Yesterdays with Authors* contains in agreeable form many of those reminiscences of men of letters and art which made him so companionable when living, and further hints of his comradery with the literary guild may be found in the memorial volume, *James T. Fields: Biographical Notes and Personal Sketches.*

Page 104, line 17.
*And one whose Arab face was tanned
By tropic sun and boreal frost.*

Bayard Taylor was in Germany when *The Tent on the Beach* was published, and he wrote back to Mr. Fields, "How pleasantly will you and I float down to posterity each holding on to the strong swimmer, J. G. W.!" After Taylor's death, Mr. Whittier wrote the lines headed *Bayard Taylor.* The Quaker origin of the two men was a subtle bond of union.

Page 109, line 9. *And fair are the sunny isles in view.*
The sunny isles in view from Great Boar's Head, and Little Boar's Head as well, are the famous Isles of Shoals, whose praises have been sung so well by Celia Thaxter.

Page 110, line 23.
*Till the huts and the flakes on Star seemed nigh,
And they lost the scent of the pines of Rye.*

Star Island, occupied then as now by fisher folk, is one of the Isles of Shoals. The township of Rye with its odorous pine-woods reaches to the sea at Rye Beach.

Page 113, line 20. *"Amen!" said Father Bachiler.*
Evidence found in favor of the Rev. Stephen Bachiler, an ancestor of the poet, after the poem was first printed, led Whittier to modify lines which implied the guilt of the clergyman.

Page 123, line 20. *His Crimean camp-song hints to us.*
The reference is to Bayard Taylor's poem, *The Song of the Camp.*

Page 149. THE PALATINE The legend on which this ballad is founded was told to Mr. Whittier by his friend, Joseph P. Hazard, of Newport, R. I., two years before the poem was written. About two years after it was published, he received a curious letter from Mr. Benjamin Corydon, of Napoli, N. Y., then in the ninety-second year of his age, who wrote : —

"The Palatine was a ship that was driven upon Block Island, in a storm, more than a hundred years ago. Her people had just got ashore, and were on their knees thanking God for saving them from drowning, when the Islanders rushed upon them and murdered them all. That was a little more than the Almighty could stand, so He sent the Fire or Phantom Ship, to let them know He had not forgotten their wickedness. She was seen once a year on the same night of the year on which the murders occurred, as long as any of the wreckers were living ; but never after all were dead. I must have seen her eight or ten times — perhaps more — in my early days. It is seventy years or more since she was last seen. My father lived right opposite Block Island, on the mainland, so we had a fair view of her as she passed down by the island ; then she would disappear. She resembled a full-rigged ship, with her sails all set and all ablaze. It was the grandest sight I ever saw in all my life. I know of only two living who ever saw her, — Benjamin L. Knowles, of Rhode Island, now ninety four years old, and myself, now in my ninety-second year."

www.ingramcontent.com/pod-product-compliance
Lightning Source LLC
Chambersburg PA
CBHW011958150426
43201CB00018B/2328